Service Industries in Regional Development

by
William J. Coffey and James J. McRae

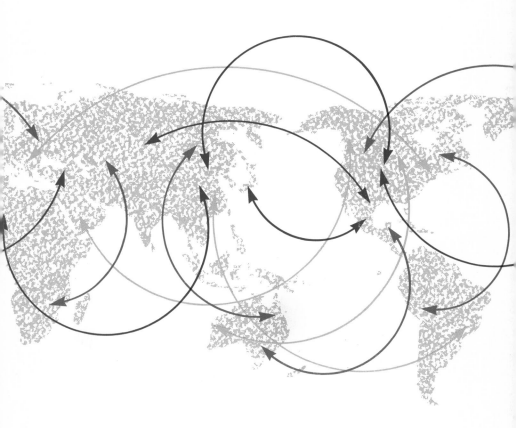

The Institute for Research on Public Policy
L'Institut de recherches politiques

A national, independent, research organization
Un organisme de recherche national et indépendant

Founded in 1972, The Institute for Research on Public Policy is a national organization whose independence and autonomy are ensured by the revenues of an endowment fund which is supported by the federal and provincial governments and by the private sector. In addition, the Institute receives grants and contracts from governments, corporations and foundations to carry out specific research projects.

The *raison d'être* of the Institute is threefold:

- To act as a catalyst within the national community by helping to facilitate informed public debate on issues of major public interest
- To stimulate participation by all segments of the national community in the process that leads to public policy making
- To find practical solutions to important public policy problems, thus aiding in the development of sound public policies.

The Institute operates in a decentralized way, employing researchers located across Canada. This ensures that research undertaken will include contributions from all regions of the country.

Wherever possible, the Institute will try to promote public understanding of, and discussion on, issues of national importance, with clarity and impartiality. Conclusions or recommendations in the Institute's publications are solely those of the author and should not be attributed to the Board of Directors or contributors to the Institute.

The president bears final responsibility for the decision to publish a manuscript under the Institute's imprint. In reaching this decision, he is advised on the accuracy and objectivity of a manuscript by both Institute staff and outside reviewers. Publication of a manuscript signifies that it is deemed to be a competent treatment of a subject worthy of public consideration.

Service Industries in Regional Development

Service Industries in Regional Development

by

William J. Coffey
and
James J. McRae

With the collaboration of

Martine M. Desbois
and
Mario Polèse

The Institute for Research on Public Policy
L'Institut de recherches politiques

HD
9985
C32
C64
1989

Printed in Canada

Legal Deposit Fourth Quarter
Bibliothèque nationale du Québec

Canadian Cataloguing in Publication Data

Coffey, William J., 1948-

Service industries in regional development

Prefatory material in English and French.
ISBN 0-88645-103-5

1. Service industries—Canada.   2. Regional
planning—Canada.   3. Regional planning—
Government policy—Canada.   I. McRae,
James J. (James John), date.   II. Institute
for Research on Public Policy.   III. Title.

HD9985.C22C63   1990   338.4'7'000971   C90-097518-0

Publication management and camera-ready copy by
PDS Research Publishing Services Ltd.
P.O. Box 3296
Halifax, Nova Scotia B3J 3H7

Published by
The Institute for Research on Public Policy
L'Institut de recherches politiques
P.O. Box 3670 South
Halifax, Nova Scotia B3J 3K6

Table of Contents

List of Figures and Tables

Foreword

It is becoming widely recognized that many consumer services previously generated within the household have migrated into the marketplace. Similarly many activities which might best be viewed as personal and social investment, and previously were undertaken within the family unit, now show up in our social accounts as health care, education, and social services provided through the public sector. And many services previously offered as internal activities within the hierarchy of organizations in primary or secondary industries now are marketed formally by service enterprises whose revenues therefore appear as part of the output of a formal service sector.

Thus the measured scale of the service sector grows, and many new activities come within the scope of public policies affecting market transactions.

Moreover, technological change increasingly makes possible a process of intermediation in service activities—a separation in space or time of the ultimate recipient of services from the original producer of those services. "Value-added" services along the way introduce new actors into the process of service provision, and the possibility of trade in such services across national boundaries brings within the scope of international negotiations and rules a vast range of activities previously missing from the trade policy arena.

Further, the nature of service activities moves trade away from a model of separated individual transactions and toward a structure of sustained relationships. The analysis of economic decisions, and of the possible impacts of public policy upon those decisions, becomes a very different and challenging exercise in these circumstances.

The growth of service activities based on such new technologies and more diverse, flexible organizational structures also introduces dramatically different approaches to competition and comparative advantage in international trade.

In place of strategies based on standardized products exploiting economies of scale in a settled organization of production, service-intensive, flexible production systems open up possibilities for global competition on the basis of custom services offered by flexible and adaptive organizations exploiting economies of scope in the utilization of a knowledge base and management skills.

Thus social investment in the creation and diffusion of knowledge, in education and training, is seen as a fruitful and productive investment—not just frivolous public consumption—and human capital is recognized as a durable asset on which longer term relationships in the organization of labour must be built. Comparative advantage in the international trading system is likely to reflect the extent of this knowledge base, the growth of human capital endowments, and the effectiveness of these organizational arrangements with the labour force.

Comparative advantage and competitive position in these circumstances are therefore likely to be ephemeral and heavily dependent on continued social investment in learning and adaptation, as well as in the maintenance of the renewable resource base and a healthy ecological system.

Anticipating the need for greater analysis of these developments, Industry, Science and Technology Canada (formerly the Department of Regional Industrial Expansion) in 1984 initiated discussions with the Institute for Research on Public Policy. Following some preliminary work undertaken by the Institute, the Department launched in May 1986 the Service Industries Studies Program (SISP) aimed at investigating the structure and dynamics of the service sector and its component industries. The Institute contributed to that program by focusing its research on Canada's international trade in services, while the Fraser Institute was asked to undertake a comprehensive examination of the growth of the service sector in the Canadian economy, and Statistics Canada was commissioned to review and develop the relevant underlying database. Industry, Science and Technology Canada will continue to work to develop a better understanding of the role of the service sector in the economy and to promote policies and programs in support of the international competitiveness of Canada's service industries.

The research program set up by IRPP was organized under four research modules, each dealing with a different aspect of the overall problem.

The first module, Trade in Services: A Theoretical Perspective, explored the various branches of economic theory to determine the positive and normative aspects of trade in services. Since the neo-classical trade and investment model was originally developed for analyzing goods trade, the research under this module was directed at identifying and exploring the various economic characteristics of services trade that must be incorporated into theoretical analysis of trade in services.

The second module, The Service Sector and Regional Balance, recognized that the extension of marketed services into broader inter-regional trade is a step—conceptually, if not chronologically—in the process leading to international trade, and therefore explored the role played by the service sector in the growth of regional economies.

The third module consisted of a series of case studies and dealt with the statistical and empirical issues encountered in analyzing trade in specific services. Transportation, financial services, computer and telecommunications, engineering services and real estate development and management were studied to explore the determinants of competitive position. These analyses were complemented by an exploration of the data already available on trade in services and foreign investment.

The fourth and last research module examined legal, institutional and negotiating issues particular to trade in services.

The present volume emerges from the second component of this work program. As the relative shift away from manufacturing and towards service industries becomes ever more obvious in terms of Canadian employment levels—and to a lesser extent in terms of output—it becomes necessary to re-examine from the new perspective of a more service-oriented economy some traditional questions of regional economics.

The notion of balanced regional development has been—implicitly or explicitly—a key objective of national policy since Confederation. The role of service industries in the process of regional and urban development is, however, still poorly understood, and still largely dominated by the concept that services are an outgrowth of surpluses created in the goods producing industries, and hence not suitable as a foundation for regional development.

The present study—which synthesizes research work undertaken by Professors Coffey and McRae both independently and in conjunction with several others over a number of years—contains three distinct elements. First a conceptual analysis of the locational characteristics of service industries is set out. Second, a detailed empirical analysis of the service sector in Canada using employment and occupational data from the 1971 and 1981 censuses, and questionnaire results obtained from service producing establishments, is summarized. Finally, an analysis of the policy issues relevant to service industries in regional development, especially the limited role of policy variables in decentralizing the so-called "propulsive" service industries away from the large urban centres or their immediate suburbs, is developed.

The somewhat discouraging conclusion from this last body of work is that while the new technologies and more flexible organizational structures associated with the service sector offer in principle many opportunities for substantial decentralization of economic activity, in fact the practical possibilities are much more limited. Transitions to a service economy will not, it appears, provide ready solutions to the problems of achieving either a more competitive regional economy or greater regional balance.

The financial support of the Government of Canada for the initiation and conduct of this research program is gratefully acknowledged. Related publications from the program are listed at the back of this volume.

Rod Dobell, President   December 1989

Avant-propos

On se rend de plus en plus compte qu'un grand nombre de services aux consommateurs, qui autrefois étaient l'affaire des ménages, sont en train de devenir un des éléments de l'économie de marché. Similairement, beaucoup d'activités qu'on aurait pu qualifier d'investissement personnel et social, et qui comme tel relevaient de la responsabilité de la cellule familiale, apparaissent maintenant dans les dépenses publiques aux chapitres de la santé, de l'éducation et des autres services sociaux. Et beaucoup d'autres services, auparavant considérés comme partie intégrante des activités de fonctionnement des industries primaires et secondaires, sont actuellement l'objet du commerce d'entreprises de services dont les revenus apparaissent, par conséquent, comme inclus dans la production d'un secteur officiel des services.

Ainsi la dimension quantifiable du secteur des services est en pleine croissance, et de nombreuses activités nouvelles entrent dans le domaine de compétence de la législation relative aux transactions de l'économie de marché.

Les changements technologiques, qui plus est, facilitent de plus en plus le processus de médiation dans les activités de services et par conséquent la séparation dans l'espace et dans le temps entre celui qui fournit originellement le service et celui qui en est le bénéficiaire final. Les services avec "valeur ajoutée" introduisent tout au long de la chaîne de nouveaux participants dans le processus de prestation de services, et la possibilité du commerce de ces services entre les pays ouvre la voie aux négociations internationales et régit un vaste éventail d'activités inconnues jusqu'ici dans ce domaine.

La nature particulière des activités de services contribue à éloigner le commerce d'un modèle de transactions individuelles indépendantes pour le rapprocher d'une structure relationnelle consolidée. L'analyse des décisions économiques et des conséquences possibles d'une politique officielle sur ces décisions devient, dans ces circonstances, un exercice très différent et qui demande une nouvelle approche.

La croissance des activités de services dérivant de ces nouvelles technologies et de structures organisationnelles plus différenciées et plus souples entraîne un changement considérable dans les attitudes vis-à-vis de la concurrence et de l'avantage comparatif en commerce international.

En remplacement des stratégies de standardisation de produits mettant à profit des économies d'échelle au sein d'une organisation de production bien établie, les systèmes axés principalement sur les services et sur une production adaptée aux circonstances ouvrent de nouvelles possibilités sur le plan mondial. Les entreprises innovatrices et prêtes à s'adapter au marché peuvent offrir des services sur mesure, employant les économies d'échelle qui mettent à profit leur base de connaissances solide et les compétences administratives de leur personnel de direction.

Ainsi, les investissements sociaux en matière de création et de diffusion des connaissances, dans les domaines de l'enseignement et de la formation professionnelle, peuvent-ils être considérés comme des investissements productifs et non pas simplement comme des dépenses publiques sans signification. Le capital humain est reconnu comme un bien durable à partir duquel doit s'élaborer, dans l'organisation du travail, un système de relations à plus long terme. L'avantage relatif sur le plan du commerce international a toutes les chances d'être fonction de cette base de connaissances, de la croissance de ces ressources humaines et de l'efficacité des rapports d'organisation avec le monde du travail.

Dans ces circonstances, l'avantage relatif et la position avantageuse d'une économie face à la concurrence seront vraisemblablement de courte durée et dépendront largement du renouvellement des investissements sociaux dans les domaines de l'apprentissage, de l'adaptation et de l'entretien des ressources renouvelables et d'un système écologique équilibré.

Dès 1984, prévoyant qu'il serait bientôt nécessaire de procéder à une analyse plus approfondie de ces nouvelles tendances, Industrie, Sciences et Technologie Canada (anciennement le ministère de l'Expansion industrielle régionale) prenait contact avec l'IRP pour discuter de cette question. À la suite de quelques travaux préliminaires entrepris par l'Institut, le ministère inaugurait en mai 1986 le Programme d'études sur les industries de services, dont le but était d'étudier la structure et la dynamique de ce secteur et des industries qui le composent. L'Institut a collaboré à ce programme en orientant plus particulièrement ses recherches sur le commerce international des services du Canada, alors que l'Institut Fraser entreprenait, de son côté, l'examen complet de la croissance du secteur des services dans l'économie canadienne et que Statistique Canada était chargé de revoir et d'améliorer la base de données fondamentale. Industrie, Sciences et Technologie Canada persévérera dans ses efforts pour améliorer la compréhension du rôle du secteur des services dans l'économie et pour promouvoir les politiques et les programmes afin d'appuyer la compétitivité internationale des industries de services canadiennes.

Le programme de recherches mis sur pied par l'IRP a été réparti en quatre modules portant chacun sur un aspect particulier du problème général.

Le premier, intitulé "Commerce des services : une perspective théorique", a été consacré à l'exploration des diverses branches de la théorie économique, afin de déterminer les aspects positifs et normatifs du commerce des services. Étant donné que le modèle néo-classique pour le commerce et les investissements était, à l'origine, destiné à l'étude du commerce des biens, les recherches dans le cadre de ce module ont visé à préciser et à identifier les diverses caractéristiques économiques du commerce des services qui pourraient être incorporées à l'analyse théorique de celui-ci.

Le second module, intitulé "Le secteur des services et l'équilibre régional", est parti de l'idée que la commercialisation des services à l'échelon interrégional était un premier pas, théoriquement sinon chronologiquement, vers l'internationalisation de ce commerce. Les recherches ont donc porté sur le rôle joué par le secteur des services dans la croissance des économies régionales.

Le troisième module a eu pour objectif l'étude d'une série de cas particuliers et des questions statistiques et empiriques qui se posaient au cours de l'analyse du commerce dans certains secteurs de services. Les transports, les services financiers, l'informatique et les télécommunications, l'ingénierie, l'expansion et la gestion de l'immobilier ont été examinés afin d'identifier quels facteurs déterminants permettaient l'accès à une situation concurrentielle. Ces analyses ont été complétées par une révision des données préalablement disponibles en matière de commerce des services et d'investissements étrangers.

Le quatrième et dernier module a été consacré à l'examen de questions particulières au commerce des services relativement à la législation, aux institutions et aux négociations.

Ce volume est le résultat du second module de ce programme de travail. Alors que la transition de l'industrie manufacturière vers l'industrie des services devient de plus en plus évidente en ce qui a trait aux niveaux de l'emploi au Canada, et, d'une manière moins visible, à la production, il devient nécessaire de réexaminer quelques unes des questions traditionnelles d'économie régionale, en se plaçant du point de vue de cette nouvelle économie, davantage orientée vers les services.

La notion de développement régional équilibré a été, implicitement ou explicitement, un des objectifs principaux de la politique nationale depuis l'établissement de la Confédération. Le rôle des industries de services dans le processus de développement régional et urbain est, toutefois, encore mal compris, et il continue à être dominé par le concept selon lequel les services ne sont que le résultat des surplus créés par les industries de production de marchandises, et qu'ils ne peuvent, par conséquent, constituer une base adéquate pour le développement régional.

La présente étude est une synthèse des travaux de recherche entrepris par les professeurs Coffey et McRae qui, pendant plusieurs années, y ont travaillé soit indépendamment, soit avec plusieurs autres chercheurs; elle peut se diviser en trois parties distinctes. La première est une analyse conceptuelle des caractéristiques d'implantation des industries de services. La seconde est une analyse empirique détaillée du secteur des services au Canada, basée sur une synthèse des données fournies lors des recensements de 1971 et 1981 relativement à l'emploi et aux professions, ainsi que sur les résultats de questionnaires envoyés à des entreprises de services. La troisième est une analyse des questions de politique se rapportant aux industries de services dans le cadre du développement régional, et plus précisément du rôle limité que jouent les variables politiques dans la décentralisation de ce qu'on appelle les industries de services "d'entraînement", en ce qui a trait à leur éloignement des grands centres urbains ou de leurs proches banlieues.

La conclusion de cette dernière partie est plutôt décourageante. En effet, bien que les nouvelles technologies et les structures organisationnelles plus souples associées au secteur des services offrent, en principe, de nombreuses possibilités de décentralisation économique, dans la réalité, les occasions pratiques s'avèrent être beaucoup plus limitées. La transition vers une économie de services n'offrira pas, semble-t-il, de solutions automatiques au problème de parvenir à une économie régionale plus concurrentielle ou à un meilleur équilibre régional.

Nous désirons, pour finir, exprimer notre reconnaissance au Gouvernement du Canada pour l'aide financière apportée dans la mise sur pied et la conduite de ce programme de recherches. La liste des autres publications issues de ce programme est publiée au dos de ce volume.

Rod Dobell, président   décembre 1989

Acknowledgements

This document, authored by Professors Coffey and McRae, is the product of an Institute for Research on Public Policy (IRPP) research program initiated and supported by Industry, Science and Technology Canada under its Service Industries Study Program. As such, it represents a compilation of original research conducted by Coffey and McRae, the results of research commissioned by the IRPP as part of the study program, and additional research performed mainly in Victoria and Montreal, which pre-dates the study program or was conducted in parallel outside of the program. The result is, we hope, a document which unites the contributions of economic geographers and economists in the frustrating but important area of service industries in regional development.

The contributions and cooperation of many people who participated in this project either directly or indirectly are gratefully acknowledged. Two individuals—Mario Polèse and Martine Desbois—participated so often and closely that their contributions can only be properly recognized by including them on the title page. Many of the data presented and the ideas developed in this monograph have their basis in research conducted jointly with Professor Polèse and Ms. Desbois. Professor Coffey especially would like to acknowledge his intellectual debt to Mario Polèse, a long-time collaborator and perceptive student of the role of service industries in economic development. Both authors would like to thank Professor William Beyers and one other anonymous referee for their extremely helpful suggestions on the draft version of this manuscript.

In addition to these individuals, several others have offered helpful advice and assistance over the years. Dennis de Melto, Jane Billings and Radek Bandzierz co-ordinated the project for Industry, Science and Technology Canada, and contributed in terms of organization, background material and helpful comments on the structure of the report. David Emerson, formerly with the Government of British Columbia, and Paul Reed of Statistics Canada, plus Elaine Kozak, Louis McNabb, Douglas Herman and Chris Lawless were indispensable in arranging for, and commenting upon, the survey of Vancouver based service establishments. Tom Hutton of the City of Vancouver and Tom Courchene from Queen's University also provided helpful comments on this chapter.

Finally, the document would not have been possible without the assistance of Robert Fullum in managing data files and compiling statistical tables, and Heather Neufeld and Connie Niblock in providing nearly flawless typed output.

Chapter 1

Introduction and Overview

1.1 The Non-Industrial Revolution

As the relative shift away from manufacturing and towards service industries becomes ever more obvious in terms of employment—and to a slightly lesser extent in terms of output—it is becoming commonplace for knowledgeable observers to debate the advantages and disadvantages of a more service oriented economy. Those who argue that the transition may be painful, but certainly not catastrophic, dub this the Second (Non-Industrial) Revolution. The first Industrial Revolution shifted the economic base of western economies from agriculture towards industry, and the Second Revolution is simply the next phase of this evolution towards a service dominated economy. Others argue that service industries are inherently unproductive, and can contribute nothing to the process of economic growth. The analogy used by these observers involves a hypothetical nation of doctors and lawyers, one group providing heart transplants and the other suing for malpractice!

Both sides at least agree on the evidence presented. The service sector in Canada is both large and rapidly growing. Measured in terms of employment in 1981, the service sector is over twice as large (67.7 percent) as the primary, construction and manufacturing sectors (32.3 percent). In absolute numbers, there were 3.28 million workers employed in the goods producing (primary, manufacturing and

1

construction) industries, and 6.88 million employed in service producing industries ranging from transportation to public administration. In fact, there are more people employed in the retail trade and
consumer services (restaurants, hotels, dry-cleaning etc.) sectors than
in all manufacturing industries. More than the absolute size of service
sector employment, it is the rapid growth which has served to focus
professional analysis and public opinion on the service sector. In
Canada, between the census years of 1971 and 1981, employment in
goods producing industries increased by 749,000, an increase of 29.6
percent. Equivalent figures for service sector employment show a
growth rate of 59.0 percent, representing 2.56 million new jobs.
Further, census data reveal that this large growth in service sector
employment was very broad based. Data contained in Chapter 2 will
show that when the service sector is divided into 10 sub-sectors,[1] each
of the sub-sectors individually posted a higher growth rate than the
goods sector. Rates of employment increase over the period 1971 to
1981 ranged from 38.6 percent for the transportation sector to 141.2
percent for producer services. Thus, in terms of employment, the
service sector is both larger and more rapidly growing than the goods
producing sector, and has given rise to the documented relative decline
in the goods industry employment.

Empirical observations such as these have generated hypotheses,
which, if borne out, are so fundamental in their impact, that nearly
every aspect of postwar Canadian economic performance can be
questioned regarding its relevance to the future. Will a more service
oriented economy generate a bifurcation in the labour markets with a
few holding well-paid, prestigious jobs and many having low-wage
employment with little security and limited chance of promotion?
What effects will the continued rapid growth of service employment
and output have on the level of tax revenue, and the operation of the
nation's social programs? Will Canada be able to compete in world,
and bilateral Canada-U.S. trading systems, in which cross border
service transactions may become more relevant due to technological
advances, organizational changes and legislated market access
provisions? What are the implications of a more service oriented
economy for the regional location of employment, and levels of regional
per capita income? It is this spatial question of whether or not a
service economy implies a more centralized production pattern which
is the main subject of the present analysis.

1.2 Overview of the Study

Chapter 2 presents a broad empirical picture of the national, regional
and urban structure of the Canadian economy. Working mainly with
census year employment data, this Chapter documents the on-going
national shift towards employment in service producing industries,
and searches for more detailed observations by disaggregating the

service sector into 10, then 41 individual service sub-sectors. The inherent difficulty with employment statistics displayed on the basis of whether or not the industry is deemed to produce a service or a good is that many employees in the goods industries may, in fact, be performing service functions. In a similar fashion, not all workers in service industries are producing service outputs—some may be performing tasks equivalent to ones done by the majority of workers in the goods industries. One possible mechanism to produce a more exact estimate of the size and growth of the service sector when measured in terms of employment is to allocate workers to service or goods producing functions not on the basis of what output is being produced, but on the basis of the tasks being performed by the workers. To investigate the issue, this chapter also documents the size and growth of the service activities based on occupational data.

At the sub-national level, employment data are used in Chapter 2 to show the structure and growth of service industries in terms of regions. For this analysis, Canada is divided into the five traditional areas of Atlantic, Quebec, Ontario, Prairies and British Columbia. Results are presented using both the sectoral and the occupational methods of measuring the service activity. Finally, results are also presented at the urban level of disaggregation by allocating employment to one of 10 different urban types defined on the basis of population, and location relative to a major urban area. In total, this procedure created 374 "synthetic regions" which were classified as being central (within) or peripheral (beyond) with respect to a 100 km radius of a city with a population of more than 100,000 in 1981. Again, results are presented using both the sectoral and the occupational methods of measuring service activity.

Chapter 3 begins the complex process of identifying and disentangling the factors which may be causing the relative shift towards employment in service industries and occupations. The rising importance of service industries at the national level is examined in terms of three possible hypotheses based on neo-classical economic theory. When the focus of attention is shifted from the entire Canadian economy to the regional level of analysis, various possible methodologies may be employed to help understand observed events. General equilibrium modelling of regional economic behaviour at the conceptual and simulation stages has advanced to the point where service industries, modelled as non-traded goods, can be investigated in some detail. Chapter 3 provides a brief summary of this literature, and concludes that further empirical development of this approach must await appropriate interregional service flow data. A quite separate and rich research methodology which is relevant to the regional development issue is available from the work of regional economists and economic geographers. There are a variety of models which may be, or have been, used to help explain the spatial pattern of service industries, but the most relevant one is the economic base approach. Chapter 3 also briefly develops the application of economic base models to the question of service sector expansion, and compares the approach to the general equilibrium literature more common to economics.

Chapter 4 makes clear that the lack of actual data on inter-regional flows of service outputs effectively precludes the empirical testing of regional general equilibrium models involving service industries. Given this lack of interregional service data, several small surveys have been undertaken by researchers on an *ad hoc* basis. In order to quantify some of the most important dimensions of service producing establishments in Canada, detailed studies have been done for both Vancouver and Montreal. Chapter 4 develops in some detail the recently completed analysis undertaken for Vancouver. Various issues of potential policy significance are investigated by means of a mail-out and interview questionnaire to approximately 500 Vancouver service producing establishments. Issues such as the extent to which services are exported interregionally or internationally; the economic characteristics of service producing establishments in terms of their size, age, type of customers, and the factors which influenced their location in Vancouver and decision to enter export markets; and the extent and importance of interprovincial and international barriers to market access are all investigated in this chapter. Where possible, empirical conclusions on these issues are compared to results previously obtained for Montreal. Finally, the results for both Vancouver and Montreal are compared to Seattle, where a similar study was recently undertaken, and the most generalizable con-clusions from all of the city based survey results are presented in the hope that broad conclusions may be reached on a variety of topics relevant to the service sector.

Chapter 5 concludes our study of the service sector by bringing forth the regional policy implications embedded in the conceptual and empirical work on service industries. This chapter primarily evaluates whether economic policies targeted at service activities are likely to be effective instruments of regional development and, more specifically, explores some of the characteristics that could potentially enhance the impact of such policies. The central issue throughout the policy chapter concerns the "centralizing" or "decentralizing" tenden-cies of producer service industries, i.e., are producer services free of the locational constraints that have made peripheral regions relatively unattractive to investment in the traditional forms of manufacturing? Based on the conceptual and empirical results of this monograph the possibilities for the development of producer services in non-metropolitan regions seem to be limited to the following producer service sub-sectors:

- producer services that respond to the demands of local economic activities;

- producer services that respond to local public sector demand;
- standardized and routinized "back office" services;
- specialized and tradeable services which are derived from long term, local expertise in the primary or manufacturing sectors.

Finally, the chapter concludes with a brief overview of some existing European policy initiatives.

Notes

1. The sub-sectors are: transportation; communications; utilities; wholesale trade; retail trade; finance, insurance and real estate; non-profit organizations; consumer services; producer services; and public administration.

Chapter 2

Empirical Observations on the Structure of the Canadian Economy

2.1 Introduction

Policy oriented discussions of the economy generally tend to focus on the short run. Seldom in policy work is it possible to move past a discussion of this month or this quarter. Yet, implicit in any discussion of short term fluctuations in economic variables is the belief that the economy as we observe it today is basically the same as the economy of yesterday. As time goes by, small, unnoticed changes tend to accumulate slowly but steadily until they produce a major "flash point" in economic history. The absolute and percentage share in service industry output and employment, and the parallel proportional declines in the manufacturing and primary goods production and employment, have proceeded for such a long period of time that conventional explanations, and the derived policy responses, are being seriously challenged. This chapter will begin the process of understanding by presenting a broad empirical picture of the national, regional and urban based structural changes which have taken place in the Canadian economy.

Observations on the role played by the service sector to the process of national and regional economic development have had a very difficult time evolving beyond the views of Adam Smith. In his writings on the topic, Smith left no doubt that he viewed the production of service outputs as adding little or nothing to the wealth of nations. His harsh indictment of service industries was based on the observation that service outputs are non-durable in nature, and hence, he argued, could not contribute to the process of capital accumulation, and economic growth. The intellectual disinterest shown by Adam Smith was continued into the 1930s, and was only broken by the writings of Allan G.B. Fisher (1935 and 1939) and Colin Clark (1940). Fisher viewed the process of economic development from primary products towards industrial goods and services as a natural consequence of rising per capita income levels. If the income elasticity of demand for "tertiary" outputs—defined as a broad range of service activities ranging from transportation, insurance and banking to education, music and science—is higher than that for industrial and primary goods, proportionally more resources will be pulled to the tertiary sector as real income levels rise. However, it was never made clear by Fisher whether the inevitable shift towards tertiary sectors was itself a cause of economic growth, or merely a result of a process originating somewhere else in the economy. The need to identify sectors which are the source or "engine" of economic growth becomes obvious once attention passes from the theoretical to the policy formation stage. Colin Clark continued to write in the tradition of Fisher but, based on a massive cross-country comparison of economic development statistics, he started to stress a second explanation for service sector growth, i.e., that the relative expansion of service industry employment and output was caused by a lower level of productivity growth in the service industries when compared to manufacturing.

However, it has become increasingly difficult—especially in recent decades—to ignore the accumulating empirical evidence on the importance of the service sector. For example, employment in service industries[1] amounted to 69.9 percent of total Canadian employment in 1984. In terms of gross domestic product (GDP) measured in constant 1981 dollars, service industries represented 60.2 percent of total GDP in 1984. Even more impressive than the absolute size of the service sector is its relative growth. As a proportion of real GDP, services output grew from 56.4 percent in 1961 to 57.2 percent in 1971 to the reported 60.2 percent in 1984. Relative employment growth was even more dramatic, increasing from 63.1 percent of total economy employment in 1971 to 69.9 percent in 1984, a growth rate of 3.2 percent compared to 0.8 percent for the goods producing industries over the same period.

When measured over a longer time horizon, the same relative shift towards service industries, and away from manufacturing and primary industries, can be documented in terms of employment statistics. Table 2.1 shows that national employment in the service sector—defined earlier—has grown steadily since 1941. In 1981, employment in the service sector amounted to 68.4 percent of the employed Canadian labour force. Offsetting the rapid rise in service sector employment was the equally rapid relative fall in agricultural employment, and slower decline in manufacturing employment during the 40 years from 1941.

Table 2.1
Percentage Labour Force Distribution for
Canada in Census Years 1941 to 1981

Sector	Census Year				
	1941 (%)	1951 (%)	1961 (%)	1971 (%)	1981 (%)
Agriculture	24.9	15.5	9.8	5.6	4.0
Forestry		2.5	1.7	0.9	0.8
	3.4				
Fishing & Trapping		1.0	0.6	0.3	0.3
Mines, Quarries & Oil Wells	2.2	1.9	1.8	1.6	1.7
Manufacturing	22.7	24.5	21.6	19.8	18.5
Construction	5.2	6.1	6.8	6.2	6.3
Services	41.6	48.5	57.7	65.6	68.4

Source: Statistics Canada (Cat. 94-739)
          Statistics Canada (Cat. 92-925)

These statistics, and similar ones for other developed economies, have given rise to some serious analysis and, unfortunately, a good deal of uninformed speculation, concerning the emerging service sector, and the long term relationship between service and manufacturing outputs. Serious domestic economic and policy issues such as the importance of productivity differences between the service and goods sectors, the wage and occupational distribution within the service sector, the importance of part-time and non-fringe benefit workers in the service sector, and the importance of the service sector as an engine of growth for regional economies have received only limited research attention. It is the last topic—the role and importance of service industries to regional and urban growth—which is the subject of this monograph.

2.2   National Trends

The notion inherent in the original Fisher-Clark typology of economic activity—the "service sector" as a residual category composed of non-productive, population-serving activities whose nature and distribution are determined by the size, standard-of-living and distribution of the population, and the location of production facilities—has come to be regarded as an oversimplification of a highly complex phenomenon. However, any economic discussion of the role played by the service sector in the process of economic growth must re-examine the conceptual issue of defining the industries thought to produce service outputs. On this topic there is room for a good deal of discussion,[2] but unfortunately the observation by Stigler (1956, p.47) that there "exists no authoritative consensus on either the boundaries or the classification of the service industries" remains as valid today as when Stigler wrote.

Services generally tend to be defined in terms of what they are not—the economic activities of producers which do not themselves directly result in the creation or modification of physical objects. In practice, this means all activities not included in the four goods producing sectors of the economy: agriculture, mining, manufacturing and construction. Under this scheme, the service sector embraces the following sub-sectors:

- distributive services such as wholesale and retail trade, communications, transportation, and public utilities;
- producer (or business) services such as accounting, legal counsel, marketing, finance, engineering and management consulting;
- consumer services such as restaurants, hotels and resorts, laundry and dry-cleaning establishments;
- not-for-profit services such as education, health, welfare and religion;
- government services such as services offered by federal, provincial and municipal governments, and defence.

A fundamental question which arises when attempting to analyze service activities concerns the appropriate units of measurement. While the vast majority of research utilizes service employment, some measure of output is, from a conceptual point of view, often a more desirable alternative. Market value or physical quantities of output, value added or the wage bill of a service producing establishment are frequently cited possibilities. The problem with service output measures lies not only in determining the appropriate units of service output, but also in taking account of changes in service quality that in themselves contribute to modifications in the level of total output. For example in health services, advances in knowledge and in the development of new drugs, medical procedures and equipment make it possible to save lives today that would have been lost decades ago, thereby affecting the total output of health services. As a result, a simple physical measure of medical services output—say hospital beds—is not terribly useful without some correction for quality change.[3] Another aspect of the problem concerns assigning market value to a service activity, especially producer services which may be priced by "non-arms-length" market mechanisms such as transfer prices which are internal to the institution using the service.

With these two measurement issues duly noted, a more detailed examination of service sector employment growth by sector between the years 1971 and 1981 confirms the observation that employment growth in service industries has been a broad based phenomena. Table 2.2 shows that the 10 sectors of economic activity directly involving the production of services gained more than 2.55 million jobs over the period 1971 to 1981 in comparison to the 0.75 million jobs gained by the goods producing sectors. Thus, over three-quarters of the 3.3 million new employment opportunities created in Canada over this period were in the service industries, and the resulting share[4] of total service sector employment rose from 63.1 percent in 1971 to 67.7 percent in 1981. All major service sub-sectors except transportation and public administration experienced employment growth rates which exceeded the nation-wide average of 48 percent. Particularly noteworthy in terms of percentage growth rates over the decade are producer services with a growth rate of 141 percent, finance, insurance and real estate (79 percent) and consumer services (75 percent). When measured in terms of the absolute number of jobs created, these same three sectors posted impressive gains—approximately 30 percent of the total of new service sector jobs created. The non-profit and retail trade categories—large in absolute terms—were equally important in terms of new jobs created. The story which emerges from these data is a rapidly expanding service sector which is being led by the fast growing, but still relatively small, categories of producer services, finance, insurance and real estate, and consumer services. The larger categories of non-profit organizations, retail trade and public administration are growing more slowly, but still accounted for the largest proportion (51 percent) of the new service sector jobs created over the decade.

Disaggregating six of the 10 service producing sectors into their component parts produces a total of 41 individual service categories shown in Table 2.3. In the rapidly growing producer services category, all activities are characterized by very high growth rates led by computer services and management consulting. Engineering services is especially noteworthy due to its relatively large size and rapid growth—in absolute terms this sector created more new jobs than computer services and management consulting combined.

The rapid growth in the FIRE sector was led by expansion in real estate management, banks and insurance and real estate brokers. Rapid growth in these three sectors was even more impressive given the large relative size of each. In total, they produced 208,000 new jobs over the decade, representing 82 percent of the total number of new service jobs in the FIRE sector.

Table 2.2*
Employment Growth by Sector
Canada, 1971-1981

Sector	1971 Employ-ment ('000)	% Share	1981 Employ-ment ('000)	% Share	Absolute Change ('000)	% Growth 1971/81
Goods	2,526	36.9	3,275	32.3	749	29.6
Services	4,328	63.1	6,881	67.7	2,553	59.0
Transportation	355	5.2	493	4.9	137	38.6
Communications	142	2.1	227	2.2	85	59.9
Utilities	70	1.0	115	1.1	45	62.4
Wholesale Trade	306	4.5	499	4.9	193	63.0
Retail Trade	807	11.8	1,215	12.0	408	50.4
FIRE	319	4.7	572	5.6	253	79.4
Non-profit	1,011	14.8	1,515	14.9	505	49.9
Consumer Services	581	8.5	1,017	10.0	435	74.8
Producer Services	179	2.6	433	4.3	254	141.2
Public Adminis-tration	553	8.1	793	7.8	240	43.3
TOTAL	6,855	100.0	10,157	100.0	3,302	48.2

For the consumer services sector, rapid aggregate growth was sparked by the leisure services and the hotel/restaurant sectors. In fact, the most important observation contained in these disaggregated data is that growth in both percentage and absolute terms is due to rapid growth in the already large hotel/restaurant sector.

The transportation sector displays wide differences in intra-sectoral growth rates over the decade. In percentage terms, the air sector displayed the most impressive growth rate, and was responsible for the creation of 27,000 new jobs. The absolutely larger trucking and urban transportation sectors grew less rapidly, but collectively were responsible for 71 percent of the new transportation jobs created over the decade.

---

* Unless otherwise indicated, all tables in Chapter 2 have been compiled using special runs of data from the 1971 and 1981 censuses. Boundary changes in spatial units between the two census years have been controlled so as to render the data directly comparable.

Table 2.3
Disaggregated Service Sector Employment Growth
Canada, 1971-1981

Sector	1971 Employment ('000)	% Share*	1981 Employment ('000)	% Share*	Absolute Change ('000)	% Growth 1971/81
Transportation						
Truck	93	2.2	134	1.9	41	42.9
Air	30	0.7	57	0.8	27	91.8
Rail	95	2.2	100	1.5	5	5.9
Marine	31	0.7	32	0.5	1	5.0
Urban	94	2.2	150	2.2	56	59.3
Storage	13	0.3	20	0.3	7	52.4
Communications	142	3.3	227	3.3	85	59.9
Utilities	70	1.6	115	1.7	45	62.4
Wholesale Trade	306	7.1	499	7.3	193	63.0
Retail Trade	807	18.7	1,215	17.7	408	50.4
FIRE						
Banks	119	2.7	234	3.4	115	97.2
Other Credit	15	0.3	18	0.3	3	22.7
Stock Broker	13	0.3	21	0.3	8	62.6
Holding Company	18	0.4	20	0.3	2	6.8
Insurance Company	64	1.5	96	1.4	32	49.6
Insurance/Real Estate Agent	62	1.4	106	1.5	44	72.0
Real Estate Management	28	0.6	77	1.1	49	173.0
Non-profit						
Higher Education	89	2.1	126	1.8	37	41.6
Other Teaching	426	9.8	570	8.3	144	33.8
Medical	405	9.4	626	9.1	221	54.7
Social	52	1.2	138	2.0	86	162.7
Religious	39	0.9	56	0.8	17	43.5
Consumer Services						
Films	4	0.1	7	0.1	3	77.0
Leisure	52	1.2	101	1.5	49	94.6
Personal	154	3.5	157	2.3	3	2.4
Hotel/Restaurant	275	6.3	537	7.8	262	95.5
Rental	7	0.2	13	0.2	6	70.0
Miscellaneous	90	2.1	202	2.9	112	124.1

Table 2.3 (Cont'd)

Sector	1971 Employment ('000)	1971 % Share*	1981 Employment ('000)	1981 % Share*	Absolute Change ('000)	% Growth 1971/81
Producer Services						
Personnel	8	0.2	20	0.3	12	149.8
Computer	4	0.1	30	0.4	26	585.9
Security	14	0.3	31	0.4	17	128.3
Accounting	27	0.6	54	0.8	27	100.6
Advertising	13	0.3	24	0.3	11	84.9
Architectural/ Planning	6	0.1	12	0.2	6	102.1
Engineering	42	1.0	96	1.4	54	128.1
Legal	33	0.8	68	1.0	35	108.4
Management	5	0.1	25	0.4	20	427.8
Miscellaneous	28	0.7	74	1.1	46	159.5
Public Administration						
Federal	296	6.8	353	5.1	57	19.1
Provincial	133	3.1	232	3.4	99	74.6
Local	124	2.9	208	3.0	84	67.2
TOTAL SERVICE	4,328	100.0	6,881	100.0	2,553	59.0

* Percentages of service sector employment, not total employment.

Most subsectors in the large non-profit category grew at a rate below the total service sector growth rate of 59 percent, but because of the large absolute size of most subsectors in this category, the number of new jobs created was impressive. Especially noticeable is the category of medical services which posted a reasonably high growth rate on a very large base.

The implicit presumption of these statistics, that all employees working for firms in the agricultural, mining, manufacturing and construction industries are engaged in non-service work, is certainly not true. Within these sectors, many of the employees are not engaged in "transformation" activities, e.g., manufacturing, but instead are engaged in service or "transaction" occupations within an organizational structure that is classified as manufacturing. As a result, all employees—both those engaged in transformation activities and those service producers who are doing transaction type jobs—are classified as working in the goods industry. If the service activities embedded in manufacturing could be separately identified, many of the employees currently classified as working in the manufacturing sector may be reclassified as service sector employees.

One possible mechanism to produce a more robust estimate of the size of the service sector when measured in terms of employment is to allocate workers to service or goods activities not on the basis of what output is being produced, but on the basis of the tasks being performed by the workers. Thus, occupational data may be a more realistic indicator of the size of the service sector than employment based on what output is being produced. This suggestion is pursued in Table 2.4 by allocating employment to white collar (high order service) occupations, grey collar (low level service) occupations, and blue collar (goods producing) occupations.

Table 2.4
Employment Growth By Occupation
Canada, 1971-1981

Sector	1971		1981		Absolute Change ('000)	% Growth 1971/81
	Employ-ment ('000)	% Share	Employ-ment ('000)	% Share		
White Collar	1,300	19.0	2,377	23.4	1,077	82.9
MGMT	326	4.8	756	7.4	430	131.8
MEDED	617	9.0	915	9.0	298	48.4
TECH	357	5.2	706	7.0	349	97.9
Grey Collar	2,731	39.8	4,141	40.8	1,410	51.6
OFF	1,192	17.4	1,935	19.0	743	62.3
SALES	1,539	22.5	2,206	21.7	667	43.3
Blue Collar	2,825	41.2	3,640	35.8	815	28.9
RESEX	591	8.6	604	5.9	13	5.9
MANU	2,234	32.6	3,036	29.9	802	29.9
TOTAL	6,855	100.0	10,157	100.0	3,302	48.2

White collar occupations are defined to consist of three categories:

- directors, managers, administrators (MGMT);
- educational, medical and health professionals (MEDED);
- technical, social, religious and artistic occupations (TECH).

Grey collar consists of two groupings:

- office and related occupations (OFF);
- sales and service workers (SALES).

Blue collar occupations consist of:

- resource extraction and exploitation workers (RESEX)
- transformation, manufacture, assembly and repair occupations (MANU).

During the period 1971 to 1981, the proportion of persons employed in white collar occupations increased by about 4 percent to approximately 23 percent of the total Canadian workforce. This relative shift towards white collar occupations was sparked mainly by the higher than average growth rates in the managers and directors category, and in the TECH occupations. The largest sub-category of white collar occupations—educational, medical and health professionals—grew at the national average.

The proportion of persons employed in grey collar occupations increased only slightly over the decade from 39.8 percent to 40.8 percent. This slight increase was led by the higher than national average growth rate achieved by the office and related occupations category. However, due to the large size of this category, the slightly higher than average growth rate was sufficient to produce a large number of new jobs (1.4 million). This outpaced the 1.1 million jobs created in the white collar sector, and the 0.8 million new blue collar jobs created.

The proportion of persons employed in the blue collar (goods producing) occupations fell dramatically from approximately 41 percent in 1971 to 36 percent in 1981. Both sub-categories of blue collar workers showed proportional declines due to growth rates which were well below the national average of 48.2 percent. In summary service occupations constituted 64% of all employment in 1981, up from about 59 percent in 1971, while employment in goods producing occupations dropped a corresponding 5 percent from 41 percent to 36 percent. The proportion of grey collar occupations was relatively stable over the period, i.e., the net shift was principally from blue collar into white collar occupations.

As indicated in Table 2.4, service *occupations* in 1981 constituted approximately 64 percent of all employment. However, according to Table 2.2, the service producing *sectors* accounted for about 68 percent of employment. This suggests that there is not necessarily a direct relationship between service occupations and service producing sectors. It is possible that, while service functions in the goods producing sectors may, to a certain degree, be underestimated by the use of sectoral data, the extent of service functions in the service producing sectors may in turn be overestimated. Clearly, it is necessary to examine sector and occupation simultaneously in order to clarify this relationship.

Table 2.5 investigates this issue by first subdividing the goods producing sector into five sub-categories as follows:

- primary industries of agriculture, mining, forestry, fishing and trapping (PRIM);
- low value added manufacturing industries, e.g., food and beverage, clothing, furniture (MFG1);
- medium value added industries, e.g., metals, machinery, chemicals, minerals (MFG2);
- high value added industries, e.g., transportation, electrical and scientific equipment, pharmaceuticals (MFG3);
- construction (CONSTR).

This table indicates that in 1981, within the goods producing sectors as a group, 26 percent (11.2 percent plus 14.7 percent) of all employment was in service occupations, i.e. white or grey collar occupations. In terms of the location of these service occupations within the five goods producing categories, Table 2.5 shows that the primary and construction sectors are the most "pure" goods producing sectors in the sense that they have the lowest percentages of service sector jobs. In the manufacturing sectors, the medium and high value added industries (MFG2 and MFG3) both had over one-third of their total employment in service occupations. For these two manufacturing sectors, office employment was the single most important category, followed by technical and managerial occupations. The same basic pattern exists for the low value added industries (MFG1) except for the fact that service occupations are somewhat less important—slightly less than 30 percent of MFG1 employment was in service occupations. Thus, it appears from these data that the proportion of service producing occupations increases with increases in the degree of manufacturing value added, i.e., the highest value added manufacturing industries employ proportionately more service occupations.

Within the service producing sectors as a whole, 17.6 percent of employment was in blue collar occupations, with the overwhelming majority in the transformation, manufacture, assembly and repair category (MANU). Among the individual service sectors, the transportation (68.4 percent) and utilities (50.9 percent) sectors lead in blue collar occupations, followed by wholesaling (29.8 percent), communications (22.1 percent) and retailing (21.7 percent). The FIRE (3.1 percent), nonprofit (4.8 percent), and producer services (7.8 percent) sectors are the most "pure" service sectors in the sense that they exhibited the lowest levels of blue collar employment.

Over the period 1971-1981, in both goods producing and service producing sectors, the largest net shift of employment was into the white collar categories, and into the management category in particular. In the case of the goods producing sectors, this shift occurred

Table 2.5
Intrasectoral Occupation Structure
Canada, 1981 (%)

	White Collar				Grey Collar			Blue Collar			TOTAL
	MGMT	MEDED	TECH	TOTAL	OFF	SALES	TOTAL	RESEX	MANU	TOTAL	
TOTAL	6.0	0.5	4.7	11.2	10.2	4.5	14.7	17.2	56.9	74.1	100.0
Goods											
PRIM	2.6	0.7	4.4	7.7	5.1	1.5	6.6	73.8	11.9	85.7	100.0
MFG1	6.1	0.2	3.6	9.9	11.8	7.8	19.6	1.5	69.0	70.5	100.0
MFG2	8.4	0.3	7.4	16.1	13.6	5.5	19.1	0.5	64.3	64.8	100.0
MFG3	7.3	1.8	8.6	17.7	13.7	4.4	18.1	0.0	64.2	64.2	100.0
CONSTR	6.4	0.0	2.6	9.0	8.2	2.1	10.3	3.0	77.7	80.7	100.0
Services	8.1	13.1	8.0	29.2	23.3	29.9	53.2	0.6	17.0	17.6	100.0
Transportation	5.8	0.8	2.2	8.8	17.2	5.6	22.8	0.3	68.1	68.4	100.0
Communications	10.0	0.5	13.5	24.0	50.7	3.2	53.9	0.0	22.1	22.1	100.0
Utilities	7.9	0.4	17.0	25.3	20.8	3.0	23.8	0.9	50.0	50.9	100.0
Wholesale Trade	10.3	0.2	2.2	12.7	27.1	30.4	57.5	0.6	29.2	29.8	100.0
Retail Trade	3.5	1.4	1.1	6.0	22.6	49.7	72.3	0.1	21.6	21.7	100.0
FIRE	17.2	0.3	2.9	20.4	48.7	27.8	76.5	0.3	2.8	3.1	100.0
Nonprofit	4.7	55.5	8.3	68.5	13.8	12.9	26.7	0.3	4.5	4.8	100.0
Consumer Services	3.9	0.9	6.9	11.7	10.8	66.3	77.1	1.1	10.1	11.2	100.0
Producer Services	16.7	0.8	32.9	50.4	32.3	9.5	41.8	0.3	7.5	7.8	100.0
Public Administration	15.5	2.5	13.6	31.6	29.2	24.4	53.6	2.1	12.7	14.8	100.0
TOTAL	7.4	9.0	7.0	23.4	19.0	21.7	40.7	6.0	29.9	35.9	100.0

largely at the expense of the resource occupations category; in the case of the service sectors, it was at the expense of both the transformation, manufacture, assembly and repair, and sales categories.

In summary, Table 2.5 shows that there exist both service occupations in the goods producing industries and goods producing jobs in the service industries. Data from 1981 show that 26 percent of all employment in the goods producing sectors are service occupations, and the location of these service jobs is concentrated in the higher value added manufacturing sectors. For the service industries, approximately 18 percent of the occupations can be classified as blue collar or goods producing. These blue collar occupations are most heavily concentrated in the transportation and utilities sectors.

2.2.1 *Additional Information on National Trends*

A closely related analysis of occupational data from the 1971 and 1981 Census of Population has recently been performed by Hepworth (1987). The focal point of Hepworth's work is on the "information" economy, recently discussed and measured in a major study by Porat (1977) for the United States. Porat conceptually divides the economy into two "domains"—the production domain in which resources are primarily allocated to the task of transforming matter and energy, and the information domain in which resources are primarily allocated to the task of transforming information from one pattern into another. Porat developed an inventory of 422 information occupations based on the definition that an information occupation is one where the income received originates primarily in the manipulation of symbols and information. Non-information workers are defined as those in which information handling appears only in an ancillary fashion to some other task. Hepworth employs this typology of occupations for Canada to show that the share of information occupations in the labour force increased from 44.1 percent in 1971 to 48.9 percent in 1981. Although one might question the dividing line between information and non-information workers, the analysis of Hepworth confirms the significant movement towards information occupations in both the goods producing and service producing sectors of the economy.

Occupational data over a much longer time period—1870 to 1970—have also been used by Wallis and North (1986) to measure the size of the "transactions" sector in the U.S. economy. Transactions activities and occupations are defined to be the informational ones, while transformation activities and occupations are ones actually involving the transformation of physical inputs into outputs. The authors convincingly argue that the measured relative and absolute growth in the number and diversity of the transactions occupations was necessary to overcome information costs which impeded wealth and income creating economic exchanges between buyers and sellers. Information costs are thus seen to be a cost like any other to buyers and/or sellers. They occur before any exchange takes place, e.g., gathering information on prices and alternatives, ascertaining quality, determining buyers or sellers credibility; at the point of exchange, e.g., paying legal fees, purchasing title insurance; and after any exchange takes place, e.g., enforcing contract terms, monitoring performance, inspecting quality and obtaining payment. The growth in the transactions sector in the U.S. over the period 1870 to 1970—from one-quarter of GNP in 1870 to over one-half of GNP in 1970—is seen to be efficiency enhancing because it effectively reduces the transaction cost of exchange. With lower transaction costs, more mutually beneficial exchanges take place thus allowing the *potential* gains from specialization and division of labour to become *realized* gains. Economic growth is viewed as a process by which the transactions costs before, during and after exchange are reduced, thus permitting the realization of gains from greater specialization. The development of specialized banking, finance, legal and trade services are all examples of necessary developments to enhance national productivity.

Further relevant information on the size and structure of the Canadian service sector is available in Table 2.6. This table shows employment, output and capital stock data for the service and goods producing industries separately, and is taken from a recent paper by Curtis and Murthy (1988). The goods and service producing sectors are defined on the basis of gross domestic product (GDP) by industry. Thus, the primary industries plus manufacturing and construction make up the goods producing sector, and the remaining industries are in the service producing sector. The distribution of employment between the goods and service industries is based on employment by industry data. Output data are based on constant dollar GDP at factor cost, estimated by value added and aggregated to the two sectors based on industry definitions as for employment. Capital stock data are for the entire Canadian economy, including private and public sectors, and distributed to the goods and service sectors.

These data on employment and output illustrate the same fundamental point developed in Section 2.1, i.e., the service sector dominates the goods sector in terms of percentage share of both employment and output. However, this table also brings to light another issue which is far less well known. The service sector in 1967 used more of the nation's capital stock—almost 70 percent in 1967—and had a higher capital/labour ratio in comparison to the goods industries. It is conventionally assumed that the service sector in aggregate uses more labour intensive production technologies than does the goods sector. Thus, the observation based on 1967 data that services are more capital intensive than goods in terms of capital/labour and capital/output ratios comes as an extremely important observation for both theory and policy.

Table 2.6
Structural Measures of the Canadian Economy, 1967

Measure	Goods Producing Industries	Service Producing Industries	Total
Employment (%)	41.7	58.3	100
Output (% GDP)	38.9	61.1	100
Capital Stock (%)	30.6	69.4	100
Capital/Labour Ratio *	13.3	21.6	18.1
Capital/Output Ratio	1.55	2.24	1.97

* Measured in thousands of dollars of capital per worker. All dollar values are in constant 1971 dollars.

Source: Curtis and Murthy (1988)

Table 2.7, also from Curtis and Murthy, shows the growth rate of selected measures of employment, output and capital stock between the years 1967 and 1984. The employment and output indices illustrate the same point developed in Table 2.1, i.e., measured as a percentage share, the service sector is becoming more important and the goods sector less important. For example, Table 2.7 shows that the service sector's share of total employment increased by almost 66 percent from 1967 to 1984 when compared to the goods sector. Measured in terms of output shares, the service sector's share of GDP increased by 34 percent compared to the goods industries. These are important aggregate observations which have caused many commentators to suggest that the service sector by itself can be thought of as an engine of employment growth.

The share of real capital stock in the two sectors did not display the same sectoral shift as indicated by the employment and output indices. The share of total capital stock employed in the service industries remained remarkably constant over the time period in question, while capital in the goods sector displayed a modest cyclical pattern. Thus, the ratio of service sector capital to goods sector capital remained almost constant over the period 1967 to 1984. Merging these observations on capital stock, employment and output growth produces observations on the capital/labour and capital/output ratios. Given the rapid decline in the share of employment in the goods sectors, and the

Table 2.7
Selected Measures of Structural Change in Canada
1967-1984*

	1967	1973	1979	1984
Employment Measures				
a) Index of goods sector employment/total employment	100.0	86.6	80.3	72.2
b) Index of service sector employment/total employment	100.0	109.5	114.0	119.8
c) ((b)/(a)) x 100	100.0	126.5	142.0	165.9
Output Measures (GDP)				
a) Index of goods output in total output	100.0	97.7	90.1	82.8
b) Index of service output in total output	100.0	101.5	106.3	111.0
c) ((b)/(a)) x 100	100.0	103.8	118.0	134.0
Capital Stock Measures				
a) Index of goods sector capital/total capital stock	100.0	97.6	96.7	99.0
b) Index of service sector capital/total capital stock	100.0	101.1	101.4	100.4
c) ((b)/(a)) x 100	100.0	103.5	104.9	101.4
Capital/Labour Ratios				
a) Index of K/L ratio in goods sector	100.0	139.6	181.9	241.0
b) Index of K/L ratio in service sector	100.0	114.3	134.4	147.3
c) ((b)/(a)) x 100	100.0	81.9	73.9	61.1
Capital/Output Ratios				
a) Index of K/O ratio in goods sector	100.0	105.0	133.6	170.3
b) Index of K/O ratio in service sector	100.0	104.7	118.5	128.9
c) ((b)/(a)) x 100	100.0	99.7	88.9	75.7

*   All dollar values are measured in constant 1971 dollars.

Source: Curtis and Murthy (1988).

relative constancy in capital shares, it follows that the capital/labour ratio in goods production rose rapidly (141 percent) over the period 1967 to 1984. The capital/labour ratio for the service industries rose as well, but the very rapid growth in service employment generated the result that the capital/labour ratio for service industries rose by only 61 percent of that in the goods producing industries. These patterns of adjustment in capital/labour ratios between the service and goods sectors produced the result that the capital/labour ratio in the goods sector in 1984 exceeded that in the service producing sectors. Recall from Table 2.6, that in 1967 the opposite was true. Also, the relative constancy in the growth rate of capital in the two sectors combined with the falling share of goods output implies that capital/output ratios rise dramatically for the goods industries (70 percent) and less dramatically for services (29 percent).

The observations on relative growth rates for output, employment and capital may be combined to produce summary statements on the complex aggregate relationships captured by these data. The strong relative growth in service sector output, as a percentage of total goods plus service production, has been accomplished by a more or less equal rate of growth in the size of the capital stock employed in the two sectors. However, the tilt towards relatively more service output has required a dramatic increase in the share of labour employed in the service sector.

There are two possible explanations for this phenomenon. The first is that capital and labour used in the production of service sector output have a very strong complementary relationship, i.e., the increase in service sector capital dramatically increases the marginal product of service sector labour. This results in a significant rightwards shift in the demand curve for labour. A similar complementary relationship exists between capital and labour in the goods sector, but it is not as strong as for services. Thus, the demand curve for labour in the goods producing sector also shifts to the right, but not as far as for services. These data do not allow one to empirically investigate the anatomy of the relatively weaker complementary relationship between capital and labour in the service industries. However, from microeconomic theory we know it will depend upon the characteristics of the service and goods production functions, especially the relative degree of diminishing returns to labour and the elasticity of factor substitution; the price elasticity of demand for services and goods in the final product markets; and the elasticity of supply of capital for use in the goods and service sectors. Whatever the reason, the expanded use of capital in both sectors has not replaced labour, but rather has been the base for expanding the labour force in both sectors. However, for one or all of the reasons discussed above, the complementary relationship between capital and labour is relatively stronger for the service sector than for goods, i.e., at any given real wage rate, the increase in demand for service sector labour is larger than the increase in labour demand for goods production.

The second reason has less to do with the different degrees of complementarity between capital and labour in the two sectors, and more to do with the labour supply conditions, and the relative movement of real wages in services and goods production. If it can be demonstrated that the real wage of service sector labour has fallen, or risen less rapidly than labour employed in the goods industry, it follows that there will be a change in relative employment levels. The exact degree of the change depends upon the elasticity of demand for labour in the two sectors. No doubt the explanation for the large relative shift in service sector employment contains elements of both the capital to labour complementarity argument, and some changes in real wage levels between the two sectors.

Even with better and more disaggregated data, it may ultimately prove difficult to disentangle these effects, but the notion that capital growth in the service sector imparts a strong complementary employment effect to service sector labour is an important observation for regional and national employment policies. A similar finding has been produced by Picot (1986) in his study of Canadian employment growth over the period 1951 to 1981. After demonstrating that the producer services sector—consisting largely of professional services, finance, insurance and real estate organizations—was the fastest growing source of employment during all three decades from 1951 to 1981, he goes on to state that,

"the economic sectors with the highest growth rate and the largest increase in share of employment (notably, producer and consumer services) were those with productivity and technological changes that were labour-using rather than labour-saving ... A substantial number of jobs may be created in sectors with high productivity gains, but their employment growth may be relatively slow, compared with the more rapid job creation in other industries, such as consumer and producer services."

Unfortunately, given the highly aggregated nature of the data, and the complex nature of the explanations as to why the capital to labour complementary relationship appears to be stronger for service industries than for goods, further investigation of this complementarity issue may have to proceed on an industry by industry basis. However, the general observation that service sector capital has been the base for dramatically expanding the labour force in service sector production remains an important and fundamental finding for both further theoretical work and policy formulation. See Petit (1986).

2.3   Subnational Trends

2.3.1   Traditional Regions

Having examined the general nature of the structure and growth of service industries in Canada over the period 1971-1981, this section identifies the manner in which these changes manifested themselves spatially.   Table 2.8 summarizes the employment growth rates by sector and by region (Atlantic, Quebec, Ontario, Prairies, and B.C.) during the period 1971 to 1981.   This table shows that for both the goods and service producing sectors, the Prairie provinces and British Columbia experienced employment growth rates which exceeded the national average.   The Atlantic provinces and Ontario experienced below average growth rates in both sectors, and Quebec performed at approximately the national average.

Table 2.8
Growth Rates by Sector
Canadian Regions, 1971-1981

	Atlantic (%)	Quebec (%)	Ontario (%)	Prairies (%)	B.C. (%)	Canada (%)
Goods Producing:	29.5	28.6	23.8	37.1	43.5	29.6
PRIM	17.5	6.2	10.4	8.5	36.1	12.0
MFG1	55.3	32.0	29.6	40.1	32.9	33.7
MFG2	37.9	43.9	28.8	94.8	43.6	38.9
MFG3	48.2	25.1	25.9	31.6	60.8	28.0
CONSTR	6.1	29.1	17.3	108.5	64.7	39.9
Services:	50.9	60.3	50.7	71.4	71.9	59.0
Transportation	18.6	29.6	37.2	57.6	45.3	38.6
Communications	46.6	64.8	58.0	61.1	61.4	59.9
Utilities	53.4	63.7	53.1	93.3	58.4	62.4
Wholesale	51.7	70.9	57.1	73.9	58.2	63.0
Retail	40.9	55.0	42.1	61.3	61.2	50.4
FIRE	115.7	64.9	68.2	121.7	87.0	79.4
Non-profit	57.5	55.9	37.3	51.8	73.6	49.9
Consumer	67.3	73.1	72.0	83.5	78.8	74.8
Producer	138.3	107.4	128.7	237.3	152.1	141.2
Public	34.0	58.5	27.3	53.2	72.9	43.3
TOTAL	43.7	48.5	40.5	58.2	62.6	48.2

Table 2.9 displays the same regional information in terms of the absolute number of new jobs created.   In spite of having below average growth rates in service sector employment, Ontario led the five regions in terms of the absolute number of new service jobs created.   This

follows, of course, from the large size of the Ontario service sector. In comparison, the rapid percentage growth in service employment in the four western provinces manifested itself in relatively modest absolute figures.

Table 2.9
Absolute Employment Change by Sector
Canadian Regions, 1971-1981

	Atlantic ('000)	Quebec ('000)	Ontario ('000)	Prairies ('000)	B.C. ('000)	Canada** ('000)
Goods Producing:	53	174	249	169	103	749
PRIM	10	6	16	23	20	76
MFG1	31	80	82	26	28	247
MFG2	5	45	75	34	13	171
MFG3	4	16	45	5	6	75
CONSTR	3	27	32	82	35	180
Services:	180	623	874	521	349	2,553
Transportation	6	28	42	38	22	137
Communications	6	23	30	15	10	85
Utilities	3	10	16	10	4	45
Wholesale	12	48	70	41	22	193
Retail	28	102	136	83	56	408
FIRE	17	52	98	55	32	253
Non-profit	48	146	147	90	72	505
Consumer	28	102	166	80	59	435
Producer	11	48	105	56	34	254
Public	22	63	64	52	37	240
TOTAL*	232	797	1,122	690	452	3,302

* Columns may not exactly equal the total due to rounding.
** The Canada column is equal to the sum of the five regions plus the Yukon and NWT employment.

Focussing attention on the percentage of service subsector jobs created in the various regions produces Table 2.10. This table shows that employment in the rapidly growing and strategically important producer services and FIRE subsectors is disproportionately concentrated in Ontario. For example, 43 percent of Canadian producer services jobs existing in 1981 were in Ontario. This is well above Ontario's share (37.8 percent) of new service sector jobs created in 1981. In comparison, Quebec received only 21.3 percent of the producer service jobs in Canada, but 24.1 percent of all service jobs. By this measure, the Prairie and B.C. regions had proportional shares of

producer service jobs, and the Atlantic region a lower than proportional share. The same basic pattern exists for FIRE sector jobs.
Further detail may be obtained by disaggregating the 10 service
sector categories into the 41 subcategories used earlier. These tables
(not shown) illustrate that in all five regions it is computer and
management consulting services which recorded the highest rates of
growth, although these high growth rates were generally associated
with relatively modest absolute increases. In all provinces, the largest
absolute changes continue to be in the non-profit sector, especially
non-higher education teaching and medical services; consumer
services, especially occupations in the hotel and restaurant sector; and
in retail trade. The apparent concentration of producer services and
FIRE sector jobs in Ontario was led by the computer, personnel and
advertising services in the producer category. In fact, over one-half of
Canada's new jobs in these three subsectors were created in Ontario.
For the FIRE sector, stockbroker occupations were noticeable in terms
of the high proportion of new jobs (53 percent) created in Ontario.

Table 2.10
Regional Shares of Sectoral Employment
Canadian Regions, 1981

	Atlantic (%)	Quebec (%)	Ontario (%)	Prairies (%)	B.C. (%)	Canada* (%)
Goods Producing:	7.0	23.9	39.5	19.1	10.4	100.0
PRIM	9.4	15.1	23.9	40.4	10.8	100.0
MFG1	8.9	33.7	36.5	9.1	11.7	100.0
MFG2	2.9	24.1	54.8	11.3	6.9	100.0
MFG3	3.5	22.8	62.9	6.0	4.8	100.0
CONSTR	7.4	19.1	34.0	25.2	14.2	100.0
Services:	7.7	24.1	37.8	18.2	12.1	100.0
Transportation	8.0	24.6	31.6	21.2	14.4	100.0
Communication	7.9	25.7	36.3	17.9	12.1	100.0
Utilities	8.1	23.2	40.2	17.8	10.5	100.0
Wholesale	6.9	23.2	38.4	19.5	12.0	100.0
Retail	8.0	23.8	37.9	18.0	12.2	100.0
FIRE	5.5	22.9	42.0	17.4	12.1	100.0
Non-profit	8.6	26.9	35.7	17.4	11.2	100.0
Consumer	6.8	23.7	39.0	17.2	13.1	100.0
Producer	4.2	21.3	43.1	18.4	12.9	100.0
Public	10.7	21.6	37.5	18.7	11.0	100.0

*　This column is equal to the sum of the five regions, plus the Yukon and NWT.

Most other sectors had regional distributions of new jobs more or less in line with the more aggregated data used to construct Table 2.10. The exception was the high proportion of federal government jobs in the Atlantic region—14.1 percent of the total of new federal government jobs created during 1971 to 1981.

The regional distribution of employment shown in these spatially disaggregated tables tends in general to be determined by relative population size in the five regions. For most sectors, the distribution of employment is dominated by the two largest provinces, Ontario and Quebec. Table 2.11 makes explicit the relationship between regional population and employment. The first two rows of this table show the regional distribution of the Canadian population in the census years 1971 and 1981. The third row shows the percentage of the Canadian population increase captured by each of the five regions, i.e., 6.4 percent of the Canadian population increase was in the Atlantic region. The fourth row shows the same information for employment, not population, and the fifth row for service sector employment. Finally, the sixth row shows the regional distribution of 1981 service employment.

This table makes clear that Atlantic provinces and Quebec employment—both in services and across all sectors—tended to be proportionately less than the share of population. The converse is true for Ontario, the Prairie and B.C. regions where the share of service sector employment exceeded the regional share of population. In fact, Ontario maintains the largest relative excess of service employment share over population share based on 1981 census data. Some indication of the dynamics of the process can be obtained by comparing the third row (percentage distribution of population increase) to the fifth row (percentage distribution of service employment increase). These data show that service employment growth in the Prairie and B.C. regions did not keep pace with the regional share of population increase. For example, B.C. gained 20.2 percent of the increase in national population over the decade, but only 13.7 percent of the new service sector employment, and 13.7 percent of the increase in total employment. The large discrepancy between rates of population and employment growth in the B.C. region is partially explained by the relatively higher levels of unemployment which have traditionally existed in B.C., and by the demographics of the population, e.g., the high proportion of retirees. Ontario and the Atlantic region experienced service employment growth approximately equal to their population share increase, and Quebec had a significantly larger share of service employment growth than its share of Canadian population increase. Thus, Ontario, B.C. and the Prairie regions currently have a larger share of service sector employment than population, but only Ontario is maintaining this position. On the other hand, Quebec, starting from a proportionately lower service sector employment base, is rapidly expanding its share of service sector employment in excess of population growth. The Atlantic provinces also have a proportionately low level of service sector employment, and are maintaining their position.

Table 2.11
Population and Employment Shares
Canadian Regions, 1981

	Atlantic (%)	Quebec (%)	Ontario (%)	Prairies (%)	B.C. (%)	Canada* (%)
% of 1971 Canadian Population	9.5	28.0	35.7	16.4	10.1	100.0
% of 1981 Canadian Population	9.2	26.4	35.4	17.4	11.3	100.0
% of 1971-81 Canadian Population Increase	6.4	14.8	33.2	24.9	20.2	100.0
% of 1971-81 Canadian Employment Increase	7.0	24.1	34.0	20.9	13.7	100.0
% of 1971-81 Canadian Service Employment Increase	7.0	24.4	34.2	20.4	13.7	100.0
1981 share of Service Employment	7.7	24.1	37.8	18.2	12.1	100.0

* This column is equal to the sum of the five regions, plus the Yukon and NWT.

Due to the importance of this question of service sector employment and regional population size, it is desirable to introduce a measure that indicates the relative regional concentration of employment in a given sector, i.e., employment standardized by the size of the region's economy. The "location quotient" is thus introduced as an index of specialization that compares the spatial concentration of a given sector in a given region to that sector's level of concentration in a "benchmark" spatial unit—in this case the entire Canadian economy. Thus, a sector with the same level of concentration in a given region as in the benchmark system will have a value of 100. Obviously, values below 100 indicate a lower degree of concentration relative to the reference system, while those above 100 indicate a higher degree of localization.[5]

Table 2.12 presents the location quotients for the fifteen aggregated sectors—one primary, three manufacturing and one construction, plus 10 service sectors—across the five regions in 1981. In the goods producing sectors, the Atlantic provinces are seen to be specialized in primary activities and in traditional manufacturing. Quebec shows a high concentration in traditional manufacturing, while Ontario is specialized in medium and high value added manufacturing. The Prairie region, as expected, shows an extremely high concentration in the primary sector, and a less significant, but still important, concentration in construction activity. In British Columbia, construction stands out somewhat. In the service industries, these data confirm the observation that has already been made, i.e., the Atlantic provinces are specialized in the non-profit and public administration categories. Quebec shows a high concentration of non-profit service activities. Ontario, as noted in the discussion of Table 2.10, shows concentration in the two most rapidly growing service sectors, FIRE and producer services. The Prairie region stands out in transportation services, and B.C. in transportation services, consumer and producer services. Note that Ontario and B.C. have

Table 2.12
Sectoral Location Quotients,
Canadian Regions, 1981

	Atlantic	Quebec	Ontario	Prairies	B.C.
PRIM	125	63	62	219	94
MFG1	119	140	95	49	101
MFG2	38	101	143	61	60
MFG3	46	95	164	33	42
CONSTR	98	79	89	137	123
Transportation	107	103	82	115	124
Communications	105	107	95	97	105
Utilities	107	97	105	97	91
Wholesale	92	97	100	106	104
Retail	106	99	99	98	105
FIRE	73	95	110	94	105
Non-Profit	115	112	93	94	97
Consumer	91	99	102	93	114
Producer	56	89	112	100	112
Public	143	90	98	102	95

equivalent levels of concentration in producer services, and that B.C. lags only slightly behind Ontario in its concentration of FIRE services. In absolute terms however, Ontario is clearly dominant in both sectors, with employment levels approximately 3.5 times higher than in B.C.

Table 2.13 captures the dynamics of this process by showing the absolute change in location quotients between 1971 and 1981— positive values indicate a growing level of concentration over the period and negative values a decreasing level of concentration. The Atlantic provinces experienced concentration declines in seven out of 10 service categories, but significant increases in the already concentrated non-profit sector, and the underconcentrated FIRE sector. Quebec experienced important decreases in concentration in the strategically important FIRE and producer service activities. Thus, the significant growth in service employment relative to population share noted for Quebec did not occur in producer and FIRE services, but instead was in the public administration, non-profit, and wholesale trade categories. Ontario's concentration in all service sectors remained relatively stable with the exception of public administration, while the Prairies significantly increased their concentration of FIRE

Table 2.13
Change in Sectoral Location Quotients*,
Canadian Regions, 1971-1981

	Atlantic	Quebec	Ontario	Prairies	B.C.
PRIM	9	-4	2	-22	9
MFG1	20	-2	2	-1	-11
MFG2	1	3	-3	15	-4
MFG3	7	-2	6	-1	5
CONSTR	-27	-7	-12	39	8
Transportation	-14	-7	3	7	-6
Communications	-6	3	4	-6	-9
Utilities	-3	1	-1	10	-11
Wholesale	-4	4	2	0	-14
Retail	-4	3	0	0	-3
FIRE	14	-9	-1	13	-6
Non-Profit	9	4	-3	-5	5
Consumer	-1	-1	4	-2	-8
Producer	1	-15	0	24	-6
Public	-5	8	-7	0	9

* 1981LQ-1971LQ

and producer services from a base which was approximately proportional to the national average. British Columbia experienced declines
in the locational quotients for eight out of 10 service sectors, with
increases in only the public administration and non-profit sectors
which were well below their proportional values in 1971.

Data on service sector locational quotients are also available in
terms of a more detailed 41 subsector breakout. These data (not
shown) illustrate that the Atlantic region's concentration in public
administration is mainly due to federal government employment, and
that the concentration in non-profit activities is due to employment in
the religious, medical, higher education and other teaching categories.
Quebec's concentration in non-profit activities is mainly due to
religious and social services employment. The noted concentration of
Ontario in the producer services and FIRE categories is due to mainly
personnel, computer and advertising services in the producer category,
and stockbrokers and insurance employment in the FIRE category.
The Prairie region's concentration in transportation is most noticeable
in the storage and rail categories. British Columbia's concentration in
transportation is most noticeable in the marine and air subsectors; for
consumer services in the rental, and hotel/restaurant categories; and
for the producer services in the architecture/planning subcategory.

Also available, but not shown, is a more detailed version of
Table 2.13. Quebec's concentration decline in FIRE and producer
services was experienced in *all* subsectors of each category, and the
Prairie region's increase in concentration for these sectors was broad
based, occurring in all subsectors. British Columbia's noted decline in
concentration of eight of 10 service sectors was also broad based across
most subsectors in each major category.

The occupational data for white, grey and blue collar divisions
presented in Table 2.4 for Canada as a whole are also available on a
regional basis. Table 2.14 shows that for all three occupational
categories, the highest rate of job creation occurred in the two Western
regions and the lowest in Ontario. Particularly noteworthy in terms of
percentage growth rates is the management category of white collar
employment which grew well above the Canadian average in the
Prairie, B.C. and Atlantic regions. The Prairie region also showed a
very high growth rate for technical, social, religious and artistic
occupations (TECH).

As noted several times already, the percentage growth rates can
give a distorted picture of the changes taking place if the existing
employment base is particularly large or small. Tables 2.15 and 2.16
show a similar breakout of occupational data in terms of absolute
change and relative proportions. Now Ontario's low percentage
growth rate is seen to produce a large number of new jobs (1.1 million)
due to the large share of national employment in the province. In fact
34 percent of the new jobs created during the decade are in Ontario. A
similar, though less dramatic situation exists for Quebec. Both

provinces manifested shares of 1971-1981 growth which were below their 1981 share levels of 38.3 percent and 24.0 percent, while the Prairie and B.C. regions had growth shares above their 1981 share levels. The Atlantic provinces showed a growth rate almost identical to its share level. These observations imply that in terms of the absolute number of new employment opportunities, Ontario and Quebec dominate, but growth rate information over the decade shows

Table 2.14
Growth Rates by Occupation
Canadian Regions, 1971-1981

	Atlantic (%)	Quebec (%)	Ontario (%)	Prairies (%)	B.C. (%)	Canada (%)
WHITE:	81.8	76.1	71.6	106.3	110.9	82.9
MGMT	168.9	103.0	112.4	195.5	188.0	131.8
MEDED	45.9	52.7	39.7	48.7	71.7	48.4
TECH	101.5	92.1	81.7	141.8	116.1	97.9
GREY:	44.6	52.0	43.2	67.9	62.6	51.6
OFF	73.7	59.2	48.7	89.8	81.2	62.3
SALES	29.1	46.1	38.3	53.1	50.4	43.3
BLUE:	27.9	30.8	22.6	32.4	41.7	28.9
RESEX	14.4	0.3	7.0	-6.3	21.9	2.3
MANU	32.0	35.8	25.0	64.1	45.6	35.9
TOTAL	43.7	48.5	40.5	58.2	62.6	48.2

that the Prairie and B.C. regions are catching up, having started from a lower base. The Atlantic region is almost exactly holding its own. When attention is focussed on the white and grey collar jobs only, the same basic pattern is noticeable except that the Atlantic region is not quite holding its own, and Quebec has a share of growth which is almost equal to its 1981 regional share.

Further information on occupation is shown in Table 2.17. This table uses the location quotient technique to describe the relative regional concentration of employment in a given occupation. Recall that the location quotient standardizes employment by the size of a region's economy. It is seen that relative to the size of its economy, Ontario has relatively high concentrations in two classes of white collar employment—the MGMT category consisting of directors, managers and administrators, and the TECH grouping consisting of technical, social, religious and artistic occupations. Both the Atlantic and Quebec regions have above average concentrations in the educational, medical and health professionals (MEDED) category. In comparison, the two Western regions are relatively underrepresented in nearly all white collar occupations. For grey collar occupations, Ontario has a high concentration in the office and related occupations category, and B.C. and the Atlantic regions in sales and service workers.

Table 2.15
Absolute Employment Change by Occupation
Canadian Regions, 1971-1981

	Atlantic ('000)	Quebec ('000)	Ontario ('000)	Prairies ('000)	B.C. ('000)	Canada* ('000)
WHITE:	75	258	385	218	138	1,078
MGMT	29	92	161	92	53	430
MEDED	25	85	93	51	43	299
TECH	21	81	131	75	41	349
GREY:	93	336	489	294	193	1,409
OFF	53	172	259	157	100	743
SALES	40	164	230	138	94	667
BLUE:	65	203	248	177	120	816
RESEX	8	0.3	11	(16)	10	14
MANU	57	202	237	192	110	802
TOTAL**	232	797	1,122	690	452	3,302

* Equal to the sum of the five regions, plus the Yukon and the NWT.
** Totals may not add due to rounding.

Table 2.18 attempts to capture the dynamics of occupational locational change by showing the changes in location quotients between 1971 and 1981. These data show that for most white collar occupations, there has occurred a declining concentration in Ontario and Quebec, and a general increase in the Atlantic and the two western regions. The same general pattern is true for the office and related occupations subcategory of grey collar workers, while the sales category showed a net shift away from the Atlantic and B.C. regions. In summary, the two tables on level and change in occupational location quotients show that for the two categories of service occupations (white and grey collar), Ontario and Quebec have high concentrations but movement over the decade is towards an increasing concentration in the eastern and western regions.

Table 2.16
Regional Shares of Employment by Occupation
Canadian Regions, 1981

	Atlantic (%)	Quebec (%)	Ontario (%)	Prairies (%)	B.C. (%)	Canada* (%)
WHITE:	7.0	25.1	38.9	17.8	11.0	100
MGMT	6.2	24.1	40.3	18.5	10.8	100
MEDED	8.5	27.0	35.8	17.2	11.3	100
TECH	5.8	23.8	41.3	18.1	10.9	100
GREY:	7.3	23.7	39.2	17.6	12.1	100
OFF	6.5	23.9	40.9	17.1	11.5	100
SALES	8.0	23.6	37.6	18.0	12.7	100
BLUE:	8.1	23.6	37.0	19.9	11.3	100
RESEX	10.2	15.4	26.6	38.1	9.6	100
MANU	7.7	25.3	39.0	16.2	11.6	100
TOTAL	7.5	24.0	38.3	18.5	11.6	100

* Equal to the sum of the five regions, plus the Yukon and the NWT.

Table 2.17
Occupational Location Quotients,
Canadian Regions, 1981

	Atlantic	Quebec	Ontario	Prairies	B.C.
WHITE:					
MGMT	83	100	105	100	93
MEDED	113	113	93	93	98
TECH	77	99	108	98	94
GREY:					
OFF	87	100	107	93	99
SALES	106	98	98	97	110
BLUE:					
RESEX	135	64	69	206	83
MANU	103	105	102	88	100

Table 2.18
Change in Occupational Location Quotients*,
Canadian Regions, 1971-1981

	Atlantic	Quebec	Ontario	Prairies	B.C.
WHITE:					
MGMT	14	-14	-4	16	11
MEDED	2	3	-1	-6	5
TECH	4	-3	-4	12	0
GREY:					
OFF	8	-2	-4	8	2
SALES	-8	2	2	0	-5
BLUE:					
RESEX	18	-1	6	-34	7
MANU	0	0	-3	10	-2

* 1981LQ-1971LQ

2.3.2 *Synthetic Regions*

To this point, the analysis of regional service employment patterns has been conducted using the five "traditional" regions of Canada. Where the issue of regional development is concerned, it has become the convention to use this set of regionally defined units. However, a number of highly significant questions cannot be examined using this framework, in particular those related to the position of services in the urban hierarchy. For example, is service growth occurring uniformly throughout the urban hierarchy?; do certain types of services exhibit propensities to locate in places of particular sizes?; to what extent may urban-rural shifts be observed? Also, an alternative referencing system permits the examination of the distinction between true decentralization and urban deconcentration, i.e., the dispersion of activities within the urban field of large centres—an extended form of suburbanization.

In order to investigate these questions, sectoral and occupational employment data, which are available at a very disaggregated spatial scale, are pooled into 10 synthetic region types defined on the basis of two concepts:

- settlement size, or position within the urban hierarchy; and

- location relative to a major urban area.

This classification system produces the 10 region types summarized in Table 2.19. It should be noted that the terms "central" and "peripheral" designate municipal units or portions of census divisions that lie within (central) or beyond (peripheral) a 100 km radius of a larger urban area—defined as a population of over 100,000 in 1981. The 100 km radius was chosen because it may be regarded as a realistic delineation of the field of a large urban area, i.e., the zone of frequent economic contact between a city and its surrounding countryside. Region type 1, for example, includes Canada's 10 largest census metropolitan areas. See Appendix A for more detailed information on the construction and composition of these synthetic (i.e., non-contiguous) region types.

Table 2.19
Classification of Region Types

Region Type	Population	Relative Location	Number of Units
1	more than 300,000	-	10
2	100,000 - 300,000	-	16
3	50,001 - 100,000	central	11
4	50,001 - 100,000	peripheral	8
5	25,001 - 50,000	central	19
6	25,001 - 50,000	peripheral	20
7	10,001 - 25,000	central	17
8	10,001 - 25,000	peripheral	19
9	less than 10,000	central	127
10	less than 10,000	peripheral	127

Table 2.20 begins the analysis of the descriptive information related to the sectoral distribution of employment across the 10 synthetic region types. Particularly high percentage growth rates for service sector employment were recorded for both peripheral and central regions which have less than 10,000 population. These high growth rates for very small sized regions were led by the producer services and FIRE categories, with significant growth rates also recorded for utilities. All other region types—with the exception of central and peripheral regions in the 10,000 to 25,000 population category—recorded service percentage growth rates which were reasonably close to the national average both in aggregate and for individual sectors.

Table 2.20
Growth Rates by Sector
Synthetic Region Types, 1971-1981

	300+ (%)	100-300 (%)	50-100C (%)	50-100P (%)	25-50C (%)	25-50P (%)	10-25C (%)	10-25P (%)	<10C (%)	<10P (%)	Canada (%)
Goods	27.5	20.2	24.9	32.8	33.8	50.5	22.0	16.4	42.7	28.8	29.6
PRIM	55.4	9.7	25.4	21.5	22.0	58.4	5.9	15.6	2.6	4.5	12.0
MFG1	21.0	18.3	19.6	34.2	29.2	31.5	26.1	17.3	94.9	88.8	33.7
MFG2	27.8	23.5	28.7	27.2	43.9	41.2	41.0	14.5	204.9	533.2	38.9
MFG3	20.5	21.2	16.5	21.4	31.7	52.8	25.9	64.1	119.9	204.4	28.0
CONSTR	35.7	25.1	36.5	47.4	45.1	73.9	19.5	14.2	59.6	49.9	39.9
Services	54.1	45.9	49.3	57.1	51.1	66.3	39.8	35.5	108.3	94.5	59.0
TRANS	33.3	22.1	27.7	21.8	32.1	24.6	24.0	10.1	97.3	70.9	38.6
COMMUN	56.0	50.7	48.8	48.2	54.4	59.1	25.3	25.8	150.2	88.1	59.9
UTIL	45.8	49.3	19.2	45.7	52.4	44.3	48.3	16.2	307.3	144.5	62.4
WHOLE	54.8	47.8	58.0	68.8	67.3	63.7	57.6	27.4	138.6	119.4	63.0
RETAIL	46.3	42.8	49.5	53.9	56.4	73.4	42.9	45.0	66.0	65.2	50.4
FIRE	67.5	64.9	68.7	87.6	75.9	111.7	62.8	61.8	253.4	313.2	79.4
NONPROF	44.8	40.0	39.5	53.0	43.0	57.8	34.6	34.5	84.2	80.6	49.9
CONSUM	69.3	65.6	71.5	86.6	69.4	87.5	56.7	45.2	113.3	97.1	74.8
PROD	127.8	110.6	112.1	143.1	107.6	169.6	104.2	70.7	1,869.0	1,540.5	141.2
PUBLIC	36.4	27.9	32.7	35.5	23.1	51.6	18.2	22.9	115.7	109.2	43.3
TOTAL	45.8	37.8	39.5	49.6	44.3	60.8	32.5	28.5	71.5	57.7	48.2

When attention is re-focussed from percentage rates of change onto the absolute number of new service sector jobs created over the decade, Table 2.21 shows that the high rates of growth for the two smallest region types translated into a significant number of new jobs—315,000 for central regions and 268,000 for peripheral ones. Only regions in the largest population category of more than 300,000 created more new service sector jobs in total.

When these results on the total number of new service sector jobs are deflated by the number of units in each category, the observation that the very smallest region types performed well still stands up. Central regions with less than 10,000 in population generated on average 2,472 new service jobs each, and peripheral small regions produced 2,110 new service jobs. The average per unit number of service sector jobs is very large for the biggest region type (136,200) then falls continuously as region size falls, then it rises again. For the middle sized region types, i.e., the 50,000–100,000, the 25,000–50,000 and the 10,000 to 25,000, the peripheral regions created more service sector jobs per region than central ones. In summary, the location of new service sectors employment remains a large city phenomenon—65 percent of the new service jobs were created in cities with over 100,000 population, and 53 percent in cities with over 300,000 population. However, very small sized region types with less than 10,000 population were the source of a large number of new service employment opportunities in total. On a per region basis, they performed better than region types with 10,000 to 25,000 in population.

The same general pattern exists for employment growth in the goods industries except on a reduced scale. Large cities are important locations for new goods production employment, but less so than for services. Nearly 50 percent of the new goods producing jobs in Canada were located in cities with over 100,000 in population, and 42 percent in cities with over 300,000 population. Goods producing jobs per unit fall as region size decreases, then like services, take a dramatic increase for very small sized units (less than 10,000 population). In total, the small cities are important sources of new employment.

Table 2.22 shows the results of these changes on the regional shares of service and goods employment for 1981. In this census year, almost 70 percent of all service sector employment was located in region types with 100,000 or more population, and 56 percent in regions with over 300,000. These shares for large region types are down slightly from their 1971 levels. Particularly important to the largest region types are the rapidly growing FIRE and producer services categories. The importance of service employment to very small region types—both central and peripheral—is clear from the relatively large number of service sector jobs located there. Note, however, that the extremely rapid growth in producer service jobs in the small region types took place on a relatively small base.

Table 2.21
Absolute Employment Change by Sector
Synthetic Region Types, 1971-1981

	300+ ('000)	100-300 ('000)	50-100C ('000)	50-100P ('000)	25-50C ('000)	25-50P ('000)	10-25C ('000)	10-25P ('000)	<10C ('000)	<10P ('000)	Canada* ('000)
Goods	315	58	23	17	28	33	7	6	158	104	749
PRIM	35	3	2	2	3	11	0.5	2	6	11	76
MFG1	84	16	6	4	9	6	4	2	65	51	247
MFG2	79	14	8	4	7	4	2	0.7	38	15	171
MFG3	34	11	2	0.5	4	2	0.7	0.3	17	4	75
CONSTR	82	14	5	6	5	9	0.9	0.8	32	23	179
Services	1,362	285	68	65	65	82	19	23	315	268	2,553
TRANS	70	9	2	3	3	3	0.6	0.6	26	21	137
COMMUN	50	10	2	2	3	3	0.3	0.6	9	7	85
UTIL	19	5	0.7	0.9	2	1	0.3	0.2	8	8	44
WHOLE	108	18	5	5	5	5	1	0.9	27	18	193
RETAIL	201	48	15	13	15	18	4	6	47	42	407
FIRE	154	28	5	5	5	7	1	2	26	20	253
NONPROF	239	66	15	13	15	18	5	6	66	63	505
CONSUM	229	52	14	13	12	15	4	6	50	42	435
PROD	179	24	5	5	3	5	1	4	20	11	254
PUBLIC	114	25	6	5	4	8	2	2	36	37	239
TOTAL*	1,677	343	92	82	93	115	26	29	473	372	3,302
Goods Employment Growth per Unit	34,474	3,598	2,107	2,106	1,467	1,637	435	320	1,246	822	2,002
Service Employment Growth per Unit	136,200	17,813	6,182	8,125	3,421	4,100	1,118	1,211	2,472	2,110	6,826

* Columns and rows may not exactly equal the total due to rounding.

Table 2.22
Regional Shares of Sectoral Employment
Synthetic Region Types, 1981

	300+ (%)	100-300 (%)	50-100C (%)	50-100P (%)	25-50C (%)	25-50P (%)	10-25C (%)	10-25P (%)	<10C (%)	<10P (%)	Canada (%)
Goods	44.6	10.5	3.6	2.1	3.4	3.0	1.3	1.3	16.1	14.2	100.0
PRIM	13.9	5.3	1.4	1.5	2.0	4.3	1.2	2.2	31.0	37.2	100.0
MFG1	49.5	10.3	3.7	1.8	4.0	2.6	1.9	1.6	13.8	11.0	100.0
MFG2	59.2	11.6	5.9	3.1	3.9	2.2	0.9	0.9	9.3	2.9	100.0
MFG3	58.3	18.1	4.5	0.8	4.7	1.8	1.0	0.2	8.8	1.8	100.0
CONSTR	49.8	11.3	3.0	3.0	2.7	3.5	0.8	1.1	13.7	11.2	100.0
Services	56.3	13.2	3.0	2.6	2.8	3.0	1.0	1.3	8.8	8.0	100.0
TRANS	56.5	10.3	2.1	3.3	2.3	2.8	0.7	1.2	10.5	10.3	100.0
COMMUN	61.3	13.0	2.4	2.8	2.2	3.4	0.7	1.3	6.7	6.2	100.0
UTIL	51.4	12.1	3.5	2.4	3.8	3.8	0.8	1.1	9.7	11.4	100.0
WHOLE	61.1	11.4	2.6	2.7	2.5	2.4	0.8	0.8	9.3	6.4	100.0
RETAIL	52.3	13.2	3.6	2.9	3.3	3.5	1.2	1.5	9.8	8.7	100.0
FIRE	66.6	12.4	2.3	2.0	2.0	2.2	0.6	0.8	6.4	4.6	100.0
NONPROF	50.9	15.2	3.4	2.5	3.3	3.3	1.2	1.5	9.5	9.3	100.0
CONSUM	55.0	12.9	3.3	2.8	3.0	3.1	1.0	1.2	9.3	8.4	100.0
PROD	73.5	10.4	2.1	1.8	1.6	1.8	0.5	0.8	4.8	2.8	100.0
PUBLIC	54.0	14.7	3.0	2.4	2.8	3.0	1.2	1.5	8.4	9.0	100.0
TOTAL	52.6	12.3	3.2	2.4	3.0	3.0	1.1	1.3	11.2	10.0	100.0

More details can be obtained on service sector dynamics and region types when the employment data is disaggregated into the 41 service subsectors introduced earlier. These tables (not shown) show that the astronomical rates of growth experienced in individual sectors by several of the smaller regions were generally manifested in small absolute increases, while the below average growth rates of the largest metropolitan areas were translated into large absolute increases. For the majority of sectors within the strategically important FIRE and producer services categories, it is in the two largest regions where the highest proportion of employment is to be found. These disaggregated data also indicate the overwhelming locational dominance of the 300,000 and over population regions. More than three-quarters of all Canadian service employment for 10 of the 41 service sectors is located in region types with 300,000 or more population. These include air transportation, stockbrokers, holding companies, films, personnel, computer, advertising, architectural/ planning, management and miscellaneous producer services. In 36 of 41 service categories, more than one-half of all Canadian service employment is located in region types with 300,000 or more population.

Table 2.23 is similar to Table 2.11 except that it shows the distribution of total employment, service sector employment and producer service sector employment by synthetic region type instead of province. This table shows that with the exception of the more than 300,000 and less than 10,000 population categories, the shares of both total employment and service sector employment tend to closely correspond to the population shares of the region types. In the case of the 300,000 population regions, total employment, and especially service employment shares, are significantly higher than population share. For the rural regions, the opposite is true. The table also presents information on the regional shares of producer service employment. Only in the case of the 300,000 population category is the share of producer service employment superior to that of service employment. In the case of the nine other region types, the percentage of producer service employment is considerably lower than that of service employment. This phenomenon is particularly marked in the rural regions.

Table 2.24 presents a more detailed portrait of the extent of the metropolitan concentration of service employment in Canada, indicating precisely where the majority of service jobs, and high order service jobs in particular, are located. The 10 Census Metropolitan Areas presented in Table 2.24 are the individual components of synthetic region type 1 (population >300,000). We find, for example, that 50.1 percent of all Canadian service employment is located in the seven largest metropolitan centres. FIRE and producer services are even

Table 2.23
Population and Employment Shares
Synthetic Region Types, 1981

	300+ (%)	100-300 (%)	50-100C (%)	50-100P (%)	25-50C (%)	25-50P (%)	10-25C (%)	10-25P (%)	<10C (%)	<10P (%)	Canada (%)
% of 1981 Canadian population	45.5	11.6	3.1	2.4	3.0	3.0	1.1	1.4	15.5	13.4	100.0
% of 1981 total employment	52.6	12.3	3.1	2.4	3.0	3.0	1.1	1.3	11.2	10.0	100.0
% of 1971-81 total employment increase	50.8	10.4	2.7	2.5	2.8	3.5	0.8	0.9	14.3	11.3	100.0
% of 1981 service employment	56.3	13.2	3.0	2.6	2.8	3.0	1.0	1.3	8.8	8.0	100.0
% of 1971-81 service employment increase	53.3	11.2	2.7	2.6	2.6	3.2	0.7	0.9	12.3	10.5	100.0
% of 1981 producer service employment	73.5	10.4	2.1	1.8	1.5	1.8	0.5	0.8	4.8	2.8	100.0
% of 1971-1981 producer service employment increase	70.4	9.3	1.9	1.8	1.5	1.9	0.4	0.6	7.7	4.5	100.0

Table 2.24
Metropolitan Concentration of Service Employment, 1981

	Population		All Services		FIRE and Producer Services	
	% Canada	cumulative %	% national employment	cumulative %	% national employment	cumulative %
Toronto	12.3	12.3	15.8	15.8	24.4	24.4
Montreal	11.6	23.9	12.8	28.6	14.6	39.0
Vancouver	5.2	29.1	6.8	35.4	8.5	47.5
Ottawa-Hull	3.0	32.1	4.4	39.8	4.0	51.5
Edmonton	2.7	34.8	3.8	43.6	4.2	55.7
Calgary	2.4	37.2	3.3	46.9	5.3	61.0
Winnipeg	2.4	39.6	3.2	50.1	2.9	63.9
Quebec City	2.4	42.0	2.9	53.0	2.4	66.3
Hamilton	2.2	44.2	2.2	55.2	2.2	68.5
St. Catharines	1.3	45.5	1.1	56.3	1.0	69.5

more highly concentrated, with 51.5 percent of employment found in the four largest centres; 39 percent of employment is found in the Toronto and Montreal metropolitan areas alone.

Location quotients for the 15 aggregated sectors are presented for the synthetic region types in Table 2.25. In the goods producing sectors there is considerable diversity, with primary sector and traditional manufacturing employment concentrated towards the lower end of the hierarchy, and in the 25,000 to 100,000 central regions for traditional manufacturing. Medium and high value added manufacturing are generally concentrated in the upper end of the hierarchy and in the 25,000 to 50,000 central regions. Construction is concentrated in the 25,000 to 100,000 peripheral regions and rural regions, reflecting the resource development boom which occurred over the period. For service industries, the two rural regions are generally underspecialized in all sectors except utilities in rural, peripheral regions. In general, the large metropolitan areas are specialized in many service sectors, but especially the producer, FIRE and wholesale trade groups. Changes in the location quotients shown in Table 2.26 show that in general, the two rural regions were the recipients of the most significant employment shifts and the two largest region types suffered the most consistent declines in concentration.

Disaggregating the service sector data (not shown) supports the observation made earlier that the particular strengths of the largest metropolitan areas are in the areas of air transport, stockbrokers, personnel and computer services, advertising, architectural/planning services and management consulting. This disaggregated data shows essentially the same information on changes in locational quotients captured in Table 2.26. Specifically, over the period of analysis, the shift was from the largest metropolitan areas towards the two rural region types, although there remains significant differences in these region types despite the movements recorded over the decade.

Tables 2.27, 2.28 and 2.29 show the distribution and change of occupation types across the synthetic regions. Table 2.27 shows that it is principally the two rural region types and the peripheral region type in the 25,000–50,000 population category that experienced very high growth rates. However, in terms of the absolute number of new jobs created per region, the same pattern as observed in Table 2.21 is noted. Specifically, it is the largest regions which create the largest number of new white, grey and blue collar jobs. The number of new jobs created per unit in each category falls dramatically as region type moves from 300,000 and over to the 100,000 to 300,000 grouping. As region size decreases so does the number of new jobs per region until the two smallest region sizes where the number of jobs per region jumps up rather dramatically. Table 2.28 confirms that nearly 57 percent of all white collar jobs created over the decade were located in the

Table 2.25
Sectoral Location Quotients
Synthetic Region Types, 1981

	300+	100-300	50-100C	50-100P	25-50C	25-50P	10-25C	10-25P	<10C	<10P
PRIM	27	43	43	60	68	145	114	167	278	371
MFG1	94	84	116	73	132	87	174	120	123	110
MFG2	113	95	184	128	132	74	85	70	84	29
MFG3	111	148	142	31	157	59	94	14	79	18
CONSTR	95	92	95	122	89	116	79	81	123	112
TRANS	107	84	64	134	76	95	64	96	94	103
COMMUN	117	106	76	116	75	113	63	99	60	62
UTIL	98	98	110	99	127	126	72	87	87	114
WHOLE	116	92	81	110	82	82	76	63	83	64
RETAIL	100	108	114	120	111	117	110	114	87	86
FIRE	127	101	72	82	68	73	61	63	57	46
NONPROF	97	123	106	104	110	110	109	116	85	93
CONSUM	105	105	102	116	99	102	91	97	83	84
PROD	140	85	67	74	52	60	47	62	43	28
PUBLIC	103	119	94	98	92	101	116	119	75	90

Table 2.26
Change in Sectoral Location Quotients*
Synthetic Region Types, 1971-1981

	300+	100-300	50-100C	50-100P	25-50C	25-50P	10-25C	10-25P	<10C	<10P
PRIM	8	2	7	4	7	34	6	27	-73	-52
MFG1	-8	-4	-6	0	-1	-9	9	1	25	27
MFG2	-8	-4	-3	-13	8	-5	10	-4	40	22
MFG3	-5	3	-5	-2	8	5	9	5	26	10
CONSTR	-1	-4	3	5	5	15	-4	-5	-2	1
TRANS	-2	-5	-1	-20	-2	-20	0	-9	18	14
COMMUN	-1	1	-1	-10	-1	-10	-9	-10	16	6
UTIL	-9	-1	-31	-12	-5	-28	2	-18	47	33
WHOLE	-4	-2	2	3	4	-7	6	-7	17	13
RETAIL	-1	2	6	2	7	7	6	11	-4	3
FIRE	-7	-1	0	3	0	6	1	2	24	25
NONPROF	-2	0	-1	1	-2	-3	0	4	5	11
CONSUM	-2	2	4	6	0	-1	0	-4	4	5
PROD	-6	-5	-5	0	-7	2	-3	-14	37	24
PUBLIC	-3	-5	-1	-7	-12	-3	-10	-1	17	24

* 1981LQ-1971LQ

Table 2.27
Growth Rates by Occupation
Synthetic Region Types, 1971-1981

	300+ (%)	100-300 (%)	50-100C (%)	50-100P (%)	25-50C (%)	25-50P (%)	10-25C (%)	10-25P (%)	<10C (%)	<10P (%)	Canada (%)
White:	76.8	67.2	63.6	79.4	61.2	90.7	51.9	49.3	177.5	142.5	82.9
MGMT	109.9	113.9	102.8	147.5	97.4	158.1	92.1	111.4	706.9	469.5	131.8
MEDED	47.0	41.9	45.3	45.5	43.9	52.7	29.4	33.3	64.4	60.8	48.4
TECH	83.9	77.0	63.8	94.5	67.9	125.2	76.3	39.6	526.0	376.6	97.9
Grey:	45.3	39.3	45.2	52.4	49.1	66.0	37.7	33.3	107.8	94.1	51.6
OFF	50.4	48.7	54.4	63.7	60.7	83.8	59.6	56.4	196.8	207.6	62.3
SALES	40.3	32.4	38.9	45.2	42.4	55.5	27.0	20.9	72.7	59.8	43.3
Blue:	26.5	19.4	23.0	33.2	32.6	43.2	20.7	15.2	40.7	30.5	28.9
RESEX	20.7	3.6	21.0	19.5	18.2	25.5	8.1	10.5	-1.7	-2.5	2.3
MANU	26.8	20.9	23.1	34.7	34.5	47.1	23.7	16.3	81.8	73.1	35.9
TOTAL	45.8	37.8	39.5	49.6	44.3	60.8	32.5	28.5	71.5	57.7	48.2

Table 2.28
Absolute Employment Change by Occupation
Synthetic Region Types, 1971-1981

	300+ ('000)	100-300 ('000)	50-100C ('000)	50-100P ('000)	25-50C ('000)	25-50P ('000)	10-25C ('000)	10-25P ('000)	<10C ('000)	<10P ('000)	Canada* ('000)
White:	611	126	28	24	24	32	7	9	119	97	1,078
MGMT	255	48	10	9	8	11	3	4	46	35	430
MEDED	149	40	10	7	9	10	2	3	34	32	299
TECH	207	37	8	7	7	10	2	2	39	30	349
Grey:	739	153	41	37	40	48	11	13	180	147	1,409
OFF	403	80	20	17	18	23	6	8	93	75	743
SALES	336	74	21	19	22	26	6	5	87	72	667
Blue:	327	64	22	22	29	35	8	7	174	128	816
RESEX	12	1	2	1	2	4	0.6	0.8	(4)	(6)	14
MANU	315	62	21	21	27	31	7	6	178	135	802
TOTAL	1,677	343	92	82	93	115	26	29	473	372	3,302
White Collar Employment Growth per Unit	61,099	7,853	2,591	2,948	1,262	1,582	432	489	940	765	2,881
Grey Collar Employment Growth per Unit	73,888	9,591	3,717	4,592	2,110	2,423	674	691	1,414	1,155	3,768
Blue Collar Employment Growth per Unit	32,685	3,970	2,021	2,741	1,538	1,736	450	351	1,372	1,012	2,181

* Columns and rows may not exactly equal totals due to rounding.

Table 2.29
Regional Shares of Employment by Occupation
Synthetic Region Types, 1981

	300+ (%)	100-300 (%)	50-100C (%)	50-100P (%)	25-50C (%)	25-50P (%)	10-25C (%)	10-25P (%)	<10C (%)	<10P (%)	Canada (%)
White:	59.2	13.1	3.1	2.2	2.7	2.8	0.9	1.2	7.9	7.0	100.0
MGMT	64.5	11.9	2.7	2.1	2.2	2.4	0.7	1.0	7.0	5.7	100.0
MEDED	50.9	14.9	3.5	2.6	3.3	3.3	1.2	1.5	9.6	9.3	100.0
TECH	64.2	12.3	3.0	2.0	2.3	2.6	0.8	1.0	6.5	5.3	100.0
Grey:	57.3	13.1	3.2	2.6	2.9	2.9	1.0	1.3	8.4	7.3	100.0
OFF	62.2	12.6	2.9	2.3	2.5	2.6	0.8	1.1	7.2	5.8	100.0
SALES	53.0	13.7	3.4	2.8	3.3	3.3	1.2	1.4	9.3	8.7	100.0
Blue:	42.9	10.8	3.3	2.4	3.3	3.2	1.2	1.4	16.5	15.1	100.0
RESEX	11.7	5.1	1.6	1.3	2.0	3.1	1.3	1.4	34.2	38.4	100.0
MANU	49.1	11.9	3.6	2.6	3.5	3.2	1.2	1.4	13.0	10.5	100.0
TOTAL	52.6	12.3	3.2	2.4	3.0	3.0	1.1	1.3	11.2	10.0	100.0

10 units with 300,000 and more in population. The equivalent figures for grey and blue collar jobs are 52 percent and 40 percent respectively. Table 2.29 shows the effects of these changes on the distribution of white, grey and blue collar jobs across synthetic region types. Again, the tremendous importance of large cities is obvious for white and grey collar jobs.

Occupational location quotients for 1981 are presented in Table 2.30. The largest metropolitan areas have the highest concentrations of management, technical, and office occupations. Medical/educational occupations are most highly concentrated in the middle sized regions, both central and peripheral. Not too surprisingly, the resource extraction occupations are most highly concentrated in the two rural region types, while other manual occupations are most highly concentrated in the region types with less than 100,000 in population. In terms of changes over the 1971-1981 period, there appears to be a general tendency for region types to reduce their level of concentration in occupations in which they were most highly specialized in 1971, and to increase concentration levels in occupations in which they were less specialized (see Table 2.31).

2.4   Summary of Empirical Evidence

A good deal of information is embedded in the statistical tables of this chapter. In terms of the overall Canadian economy, the increasing significance of service activities is readily apparent. Over the period 1971-1981, 77.3 percent of all new jobs created were in the service sectors, bringing the 1981 share of employment in services to 67.7 percent. The producer service and FIRE groupings experienced the highest growth rates in the economy at 141.2 percent and 79.4 percent respectively. From an occupational perspective, the white and grey collar categories accounted for 75.3 percent of the total increase in employment, bringing their share of total employment to 64.2 percent in 1981. The highest growth rates are both obtained within the white collar category—management occupations at 131.8 percent and technical at 97.9 percent. Further, even within the goods producing sectors, the percentages of service occupations are quite significant.

When attention shifts from national to regional trends—using the five provincially defined regions of Atlantic, Quebec, Ontario, Prairies and British Columbia—some readjustments to the economic structure of the regions clearly occurred. These changes are related to the western provinces' resource boom and, to a lesser extent, to the flight of certain high order service firms from Quebec due to the political/cultural/linguistic uncertainties during the mid-1970s. The period may be described as one of *relative change* but *absolute stability*.

Table 2.30
Occupational Location Quotients
Synthetic Region Types, 1981

	300+	100-300	50-100C	50-100P	25-50C	25-50P	10-25C	10-25P	<10C	<10P
White:										
MGMT	123	96	85	86	73	80	66	75	62	57
MEDED	97	121	108	104	112	110	110	117	86	92
TECH	122	100	94	82	76	86	72	77	59	53
Grey:										
OFF	118	102	92	95	83	87	77	86	65	57
SALES	101	111	107	115	111	109	111	109	84	86
Blue:										
RESEX	22	41	50	54	67	102	118	112	306	383
MANU	93	97	113	108	118	107	115	106	117	105

Table 2.31
Change in Occupational Location Quotients
Synthetic Region Types, 1971-1981

	300+	100-300	50-100C	50-100P	25-50C	25-50P	10-25C	10-25P	<10C	<10P
White:										
MGMT	-11	-1	-6	5	-10	2	-5	4	42	32
MEDED	1	3	4	-3	0	-6	-3	4	-4	2
TECH	-7	-4	-13	-2	-11	4	0	-18	37	30
Grey:										
OFF	-7	-2	1	0	1	4	7	9	24	25
SALES	0	-1	3	0	2	0	-1	-3	3	4
Blue:										
RESEX	4	3	10	7	11	12	18	22	-63	-45
MANU	-5	-4	-4	-2	2	0	2	-1	16	17

While the Prairie provinces and British Columbia experienced higher growth rates and generally increasing concentrations of employment, particularly in a wide range of FIRE and producer service functions, Ontario and Quebec recorded the largest absolute increases, both for services and for goods production due to the large absolute size of these regional economies. Ontario actually increased its concentration, both absolute and relative, of computer services, advertising, air and urban transport, and personal services, while Quebec did the same in the majority of not-for-profit services. Due to their initial economic structures, Ontario and Quebec obtained considerable growth in spite of generally decreasing relative shares of service employment. The Atlantic provinces saw increasing concentrations of FIRE, not-for-profit and certain producer service employment, but they continue to lag far behind all other regions in terms of their relative concentrations of high order services.

Employment growth generally, and in the service sectors and occupations, in particular, tend to be closely related to the existing distribution of the population across regions. The largest regions experienced the greatest absolute growth. Thus Ontario and Quebec continue their domination of the Canadian economy; at least several more decades of the types of relative shifts witnessed during 1971-1981 would probably be required for this basic structure to change significantly. In sum, there is no evidence that the rapid growth in services fundamentally altered the established regional economic order during the period of analysis.

In terms of Canada's urban structure, the distribution of service employment follows a clear hierarchical pattern. High order (non-residentiary) services tend to be concentrated in the larger urban centres, while residentiary services, as would be expected, tend to follow the distribution of the population. As in the case of the traditionally defined regions, an analysis of the synthetic region types defining the Canadian urban hierarchy indicates that those units characterized by the highest growth rates—rural regions and smaller urban places—also experienced relatively small absolute growth. On the other hand, the largest metropolitan areas (300,000+) behaved in a manner analogous to Ontario, as described above, i.e., in spite of relatively modest growth rates they saw large absolute employment gains, but they experienced declines in their level of service employment concentration relative to other region types.

Earlier in the chapter, the use of a system of synthetic region types was introduced by means of three questions concerning the propensities of certain activities to locate in places of particular size, concerning the notion of an urban-rural shift, and concerning the distinction between decentralization and deconcentration. The data from this chapter allow some responses to these questions. First, in spite of net relative shifts towards other region types, in the vast majority of sectors and of occupations, the 300,000 + region types continue to dominate service employment, particularly where higher order functions were concerned. There is a clear tendency for services in general, and especially those of a high order variety, to locate in the largest centres. This tendency is far stronger than expected on the basis of population distribution alone.

Second, there is indeed a relative but not absolute change in employment away from the 300,000 + region types—and, to a lesser extent, from the 100,000–300,000 and 50,000–100,000 central types— toward the two rural region types. The extent of this change is, however, insufficient to characterize it as a major urban-rural shift. The urban region types continue to dominate by all measures. In the case of services, where shifts did occur, they appear to be directly related to changes in the location of manufacturing activity, particularly of traditional forms of manufacturing, and to increased resource development in rural areas. Further, where service shifts away from large metropolitan areas have taken place, the data indicate that they involve primarily the types of routinized and standardized activities generally referred to as "back office" functions, e.g., data processing, security services and non-strategic administrative tasks. The higher order "front office" functions, those involving strategic tasks or requiring face-to-face contact with clients, remained concentrated in the larger metropolitan areas.

Third, 53.4 percent of all employment growth that took place outside of the two largest region types occurred in central region types, as opposed to 46.6 percent in peripheral region types. This indicates that where changes took place they did so principally in such a manner as to extend the urban field of large centres (i.e., decongestion) rather than to promote differential growth in truly peripheral areas (decentralization). Where a true decentralization of employment did occur, it was largely confined to the Prairie provinces and British Columbia, and is principally a function of the resource boom in these regions during the period. The "distance effect" appears to be especially important in the location of high order service employment. Medium and smaller sized urban areas within the urban shadow of a major centre had considerable difficulty in developing high order service activities. Beyond the urban shadow, however, the ability of these smaller and medium sized centres to successfully generate a certain level of high order service activity increased. The implications of this for the growth prospects of peripheral areas is highly important. It is worth noting, however, that the 50-100 peripheral region types, i.e., those medium sized centres not in the "urban shadow" of a metropolitan area, experienced net positive regional effects. Thus, there may be some additional cause for optimism concerning the growth prospects of this region type.

On balance, during the period in question, the space-economy of the Canadian urban hierarchy may be characterized as one of relative stability—a stability that is the result of two opposing forces. On the one hand, as noted above, the growth of service activities tended to favour the concentration of employment in the largest urban centres. In spite of negative relative shifts, the continued dominance of the large centres is unquestionable. On the other hand, there has been a significant shift in goods production employment away from the largest centres—these shifts took the form of both decentralization and decongestion.

Notes

1. The definition of exactly which industries should be classified as service producing has generated a good deal of discussion. These numbers use the definition adopted by the Canadian System of National Accounts (CSNA), and as such include: transportation, storage and communication; wholesale trade; retail trade; finance and insurance; real estate operators and insurance agents; business services; government services; education services, health and social service; accommodation, food and beverage and other services. In the terms of the 1980 Standard Industrial Classification (SIC), these industries are defined as major groups 45 to 48 and 50 to 99. See Statistics Canada, *Service Industries in the Business Sector* (Volume 1).

2. For a partial list of the various classification schemes see Fuchs (1968), Gershuny (1978), Shelp (1981), Stanback et al. (1981), Gershuny and Miles (1983), and Melvin (1989).

3. Opinions on whether or not this problem is more serious for services in comparison to goods industries vary widely. See Gershuny and Miles (1983), and Kendrick (1985) for more discussion.

4. These reported shares are slightly smaller than the ones shown in Table 1.1 because they measure employment, not labour force.

5. The location quotient is defined as:

    $(e_{ir}/Er)/(e_{in}/En)$

    where: e_i = employment in a given sector, i
    E = total employment across all sectors
    r = a given region
    n = the benchmark, defined as all provinces together

Chapter 3

Service Industries in Regional and Urban Development: Some Theory

3.1 The Location of Service Activities

What factors underlie the varying locational patterns of service sub-sectors that have been observed in Chapter 2? In a regional development context this question is fundamental; it is the "why" underlying the "where"—the locational factors and constraints that characterize the spatial distribution of individual sectors of activity—that determines the impact of service growth upon spatial inequalities. While the issues of locational propensities is highly complex, certain valid generalizations can be made. Above all, the ability to explain the location of service activities rests upon the distinctions between different classes of services; perhaps the most useful distinction is one based upon user sectors.

In this section, locational tendencies relative to the traditionally defined regions shown in Tables 2.8–2.18 are generally not considered. While differences in service concentration between Toronto and a medium-sized city such as Guelph, Ontario can be addressed using a coherent body of geographical and economic theory, the fact that Canada's largest city is in Ontario rather than in Nova Scotia is a separate issue and requires a different form of analysis. Further, the present analysis remains at the level of the urban-rural continuum; the question of intrametropolitan location—the Central Business

District (CBD) vs. the suburbs—is an entirely distinct matter involving different factors and is not considered here.

3.1.1 *Public, Mixed and Final Demand Private Services*

It is first necessary to distinguish between *public* and private services. The former may be further sub-divided into two types. Not-for-profit services (education, health and welfare) are generally provided to households by various levels of government. (This is the case in Canada, but there are considerable variations between countries in terms of the level of privatization of "public" services and, consequently, in the degree to which they really are "not-for-profit"). It is therefore logical that these activities are located in proximity to the households that they serve. Table 2.25 indicates that reality reflects this logic, with the exception of an overrepresentation in the 100–300 city class (many of which are important regional university and medical centres), of a very slight underrepresentation in the 300+ cities, and of an underrepresentation in rural areas (<10,000 population); the latter underrepresentation is in fact a general phenomenon involving virtually all service classes, and may be attributed to the low population density of rural areas.

A second type of public service consists of public administration at the federal, provincial and municipal levels and national defence at the federal level. Once again, these activities generally follow the distribution of the population, particularly in the case of municipal administration. The location of this set cannot be entirely explained by the distribution of the population, however, even if there is a tendency to concentrate many administrative functions in relatively large national, provincial and regional capitals. On the one hand, certain functions may have very particular locational requirements; for example, the maritime branch of the Canadian armed forces generally needs to be located in an ocean port. On the other hand, many decisions concerning the location of public administration functions reflect neither the distribution of the population, nor considerations of economic efficiency; in many instances these activities may be regarded as indirect elements of regional development policy. Thus we find the philatelic branch of Canada Post in Antigonish, Nova Scotia and a major facility of the Department of Veterans' Affairs in Charlottetown, P.E.I. Specific physical factors may also be involved, as in the case of the location of Parks Canada activities.

Transport, utilities, communication services represent a *mixture* of government-operated activities (airports and ports; municipal transport); Crown corporations (Ontario Hydro or CNCP Telecommunications); and private services (private truck or bus firms; Bell Canada). Table 2.25 indicates that these sub-sectors are very irregularly distributed; both the wide diversity of activities and the varied patterns of ownership contribute to this locational complexity.

In certain cases these activities are in the final demand sector and locate in proximity to the population (transport of persons). In other cases, they are located in proximity to a physical feature (marine transport) or a natural resource (natural gas), or in proximity to primary or secondary activities (grain storage, transport of goods). In still other cases, the pattern may reflect certain "strategic" locations (Canadian National Railway facilities, located until recently in Moncton, the "hub" of the Atlantic provinces' land transport routes).

Where the remaining *private* services are concerned, two distinct classes may be identified. First, the location of retail and consumer services (final demand or residentiary activities) can be largely explained by the distribution of households, perhaps weighted by purchasing power. Table 2.25 (and even Table 2.12) shows this effect. The absence of these activities in rural regions and the corresponding overconcentration in small and medium-sized cities may of course be explained by reference to central place theory; the sparsely distributed rural population must travel to the closest central place in order to avail itself of these services. Consumer services, especially personal services, tend to follow the distribution of the population even more closely than do retail services. With respect to Table 2.12, it is interesting, and somewhat surprising, to note the relatively high concentration of retail services in the Atlantic provinces. This has been made possible by federal transfer payments which, rather than promoting economic development, have artificially inflated the capacity for consumer spending.

3.1.2 *The Location of Private Intermediate Demand Services*

It is the second group of private services, those principally serving intermediate demand, that are the main contributors to the spatial concentration of tertiary employment in the Canadian space economy: FIRE and producer services. From an intellectual perspective, this group provides the most fertile ground for enquiry since its locational patterns tend not to be explained by the distribution of the population, natural resources, or physical features.

A number of complementary frameworks can be utilized to explain the location of private intermediate demand services. A first involves what Illeris (1989) refers to as the "structural explanation", a term which refers to the structural effect in shift-share analysis. The basic reasoning is that since employment growth is occurring more rapidly in high order intermediate demand services and less rapidly in routine service activities, the logical result is the increased concentration of employment in large cities such as Toronto and Montreal where the most rapidly growing classes of activities are over-represented. (See last column of Table 2.2 for an indication of differences in growth rates by sector.) This is not highly satisfactory as an explanatory framework as the argument is largely circular. Further, it furnishes only a partial explanation of the increasing concentration of these activities, while neglecting the question of initial concentration. The frameworks reviewed below more directly contribute to our understanding of both initial and increasing concentration of intermediate demand services.

A second explanation is based upon the concept of agglomeration economies, or externalities. Here, the argument is that the concentration of intermediate demand services in a small number of large cities enables the transaction costs associated with the production and delivery of such services to be minimized. In particular, it is the cost of maintaining face-to-face contact between the producers and the consumers of these services that is potentially the most expensive element of intermediate service production, and the expense that can be most significantly reduced by spatial agglomeration. A well developed literature indicates that telecommunications technologies may be successfully substituted for face-to-face contact only in those cases where the information to be transmitted is relatively standardized, or if the individuals know one another intimately and trust one another fully (Gottmann 1977). In the case of negotiations, strategic discussions and other dialogical situations, face-to-face contact remains absolutely essential (Pye 1979). Thus in large cities such as Toronto and Montreal, these forces of agglomeration generally produce what has been termed a "complex of corporate activities": the spatial clustering and mutual symbiosis of (1) the head offices of primary, secondary and tertiary sector firms; (2) high order financial establishments; and (3) the high order producer services that serve the first two types, as well as other producer service firms (approximately 50 percent of all producer services serve as intermediate inputs into other service firms (Illeris 1989)). Such forces of agglomeration produce corporate complexes at the regional (Edmonton) and national (Toronto) scales, in which accessibility to the corresponding market area is maximized. In addition, the growth of international trade in producer services has encouraged their location in certain "world cities" (a status to which Toronto, Montreal and Vancouver aspire) which, due to both the convergence of airline routes and to cultural factors, have the highest levels of accessibility to other international centres.

A third framework, one of the most comprehensive explanations formulated thus far, is furnished by the simple locational model proposed by Coffey and Polèse (1987b; 1987c). This model, which adopts a microeconomic approach and which is the result of both inductive and deductive lines of enquiry, posits that in its locational decision a high order service firm (i.e., producer service or FIRE activities) will seek to minimize a production or cost function involving three factor inputs: complementary intermediate demand services, human resources, and the cost of communicating (delivering) its output. The former two elements represent externally purchased and internally provided factor inputs, respectively, and the possibility for factor substitution exists. The decision concerning this substitution between externally purchased services and internal human resources will be affected by economic factors, such as the advantages of contracting-out (vertical disintegration); in particular, the propensity to purchase services externally will be increased where non-standardized service inputs with relatively unpredictable demand are involved. The cost of each factor input and, thus, the value of the production function, will vary with location. In sum, each high order service establishment is subjected to three locational pulls: toward urban centres characterized by the availability of diversified complementary producer services; toward centres with specialized pools of skilled labour; and toward the market for its output. Certain locations, such as Toronto, Montreal or Vancouver may combine two or more of these attributes and thus will enjoy a major advantage in attracting and retaining high order service firms; a location such as Halifax, in spite of its highly skilled labour force, will be at a disadvantage with respect to these larger centres.

In terms of the third element of the model, the market for high order intermediate demand services, it is worth noting in particular that the spatial pattern of corporate ownership and control imposes a marked centralizing influence upon the location of producer service and FIRE activities. Headquarters and divisional head offices of large corporations have a high propensity to purchase from sources in their direct proximity the major proportion of those high order services consumed by their widely dispersed branch establishments. As corporate control and its associated spatial division of administrative functions tend to be highly concentrated in a small number of Canada's large metropolitan areas, it follows that the demand for these intermediate service inputs will be similarly concentrated. This phenomenon is examined in more detail in Chapter 5, as is the issue of the potential impact of telecommunications technology upon the location of intermediate demand services.

In summary, service activities, as a whole, are often perceived as being "footloose" or free of the type of locational constraints that are typically cited to explain, for example, the relative absence of manufacturing in the Atlantic provinces. While many service activities do have locational constraints, certain classes of them are characterized, at lease in theory, by a higher degree of locational flexibility than many other types of economic activities. It is precisely for this reason that services have begun to generate a high degree of interest as vehicles for stimulating economic growth in the peripheral regions of Canada.

The locational trends of all services, and intermediate demand services in particular, are most fruitfully examined in the framework of the urban-rural continuum (the synthetic regions types). In this context, we have seen that service employment is highly centralized in a small set of large cities. The disparities observed between the traditionally defined regions of Canada, those that have preoccupied Canadians to such an extent over the past 50 years, may thus in large measure be viewed as a function of the inequalities in the spatial distribution of metropolitan centres. The 10 largest metropolitan areas displayed in Table 2.24, containing approximately 56 percent of all Canadian service employment and 70 percent of all FIRE and producer service employment, are distributed across only five different provinces; six of these 10 metropolitan areas are found in Ontario and Quebec alone, along the Windsor to Quebec axis that has long been Canada's principal agglomeration of population and economic activity. Such concentration of the most rapidly growing sectors of the economy does not bode well for the development prospects of the remaining provinces and regions, those where few or no large cities are found.

3.2 The Interdependence Between Services and Goods Production

One of the principal characteristics of the evolution of modern economic systems is the increasing interdependence between services and goods production (Gershuny and Miles, 1983; Bailly and Maillat, 1988). Rather than increasing the autonomy between these two types of activities, the rapid growth of services in developed economies has caused the boundary separating them to become increasingly indistinct. The growing "tertiarization" of goods production, and the corresponding increase in the capital intensity of services are widely acknowledged phenomena (Marshall, 1988). In such circumstances, the precise dimensions of a production system can no longer be adequately represented using the sharp distinction between the manufacture of goods and the production of services.

There are two principal ways in which the interdependence between goods production and services manifests itself. *First*, goods and services are becoming increasingly complementary. The modern economies of developed countries are witnessing important trans-formations in *what* types of goods are produced, and in *how* these goods are produced (Noyelle and Stanback, 1984).

In terms of *what* is produced, there has been a marked trend toward greater product differentiation as consumers are attracted to more stylized products and as producers target special groups of consumers. The design, marketing and distribution aspects of goods production have thus become increasingly important. At the same time, many services closely related to consumption have come to the fore: maintenance, finance, and instruction. General Motors Acceptance Corporation, for example, a division of one of the United States' largest manufacturers that was originally established to assist consumers in the purchase of their motor vehicles by providing credit, has emerged as one of that country's largest financial establishments. The relation between computer hardware and software is also often cited as an example of this complementarity; neither is able to function without its counterpart.

In terms of *how* goods are produced, there has been a marked tendency to substitute high-technology-embodied capital for labour in goods producing processes (Noyelle and Stanback, 1984). This has allowed management's attention to be shifted away from physical production, where processes are increasingly routinized, toward other areas which previously had been regarded as deserving of only secondary priority: corporate and product planning, research and development, advertising and marketing, and administrative control. In addition, increases in the size and complexity of manufacturing firms and the proliferation of government regulation in many countries have necessitated the incorporation of more diversified and more advanced levels of management expertise.

Second, as Gershuny (1978) has noted, in the emerging "self-service economy" there has been a substitution effect through which manufactured goods operated by consumers have displaced certain consumer services. Washing machines and automobiles, for example, have been substituted for laundry and transportation services. At the same time, however, as previously noted, increasing service inputs have been required to market, distribute and maintain these manufactured goods.

Nowhere is the interdependence between goods production and services more evident than in the case of the set of activities referred to as producer services—those intermediate-demand functions that serve as inputs into the production of goods and of other services (and that, as such, are perhaps more correctly characterized as indirect elements of the production process). From their origins as almost exclusively administrative functions in the 1950s (marketing, accounting, advertising), producer services have more recently expanded in scope so as to include broader functions related to innovation, information and control. The strategic role played by producer services within production systems is widely recognized, based upon the contribution that they can make to promoting or facilitating overall economic change and adaptation. In an age of rapid technological change, certain producer services provide the source and mediators of that change (Marquand, 1983); they influence the adjustment of a production system in response to changing economic circumstances; and they may help to adapt skills, attitudes, products and processes to changes, or to reduce the structural, organizational, managerial and informational barriers to adjustment (Marshall, 1988).

An establishment may internalize or externalize its consumption of a given producer service input. On the one hand, the necessary function may be provided by the organization's own employees. This practice is fairly widespread; as Chapter 2 indicated, in the Canadian economy between 20 and 36 percent of employment in the major goods producing sectors involves a service function; in certain sub-sectors such as chemical products and petroleum refining the figure increases to over 50 percent. On the other hand, the firm or establishment may purchase the required input from a free-standing organization specializing in the production of such services. These free-standing producer service activities have known the highest rates of growth of any sector of developed economies, reaching 141.2 percent in Canada over the period 1971-1981 (see Chapter 2).

It is clear that the possibility exists for a given firm or establishment to substitute between these two forms of factor inputs. The use of externalized inputs is largely a function of the degree of non-standardization and the unpredictability of demand of a particular service (Coffey and Polèse, 1987b), and of attempts to achieve a higher level of production flexibility and external economies of scale (Scott, 1988). This capacity for substitution lies at the base of a debate over whether the growth of services, in general, and of producer services, in particular, is real or illusory; this controversy also includes issues concerning shifts in consumption preferences, the lower productivity of services and the lower and more flexible wages paid by service activities (Gershuny and Miles, 1983; McRae, 1985). Marshall (1988) characterizes the debate as one between the post-industrial and deindustrialization perspectives. The former view holds that the growth of service activities is a concomitant of the natural and desirable evolution of the economy in which growth is sustained by knowledge, skills and information rather than by capital. The latter view holds that service growth is neither positive nor progressive, being a result of the deindustrialization of developed economies due to new and more productive technologies and due to off-shore competition involving lower wage rates. These complex issues have not been satisfactorily resolved in the literature. Rather than attempting to address them here, we simply note that the increasing interdependence of services and goods production is a well documented phenomenon.

Even in the case of producer services, perhaps the most visible of the connections between the production of goods and the production of services, there is considerable difficulty in identifying and measuring the precise extent of the interdependence. This difficulty is related to the highly indirect channels through which producer service flows can occur (Coffey and Polèse, 1987c), to definitional and classificatory problems (Marshall, 1988), and to the more fundamental fact that conventional typologies based upon the three-sector classification reinforce the distinction between services and goods producing activities.

3.3   Why Has the Service Sector Expanded?

Stimulated in large part by the pioneering work of W. Baumol (1967, 1985a) and V. Fuchs (1968), three hypotheses have emerged to explain the rapid growth of the service sector in the postwar period.

The first possible explanation for the large relative shift toward service sector output and employment assumes that service outputs enter directly into final demand, and considered as a group, have an income elasticity of demand greater than unity. Thus, as Canadian real income per capita has increased over time, the consumption of real services per capita has grown more than the proportional growth in income. This "tilt" toward increased final demand for service outputs implies that services will consume an increasing share of national income and employment. Victor Fuchs (1968) reviewed the U.S. evidence for the period 1929 to 1965, and concludes that this explanation is theoretically valid, but empirically weak as an explanation of the increasing relative importance of services in U.S. employment. The Economic Council of Canada (1978) and S. Magun (1982) both examine this possible explanation for Canada. Although measurement problems abound, and research methodologies differ somewhat, the Canadian data also show that rising per capita income levels explain some of the relative shift toward service outputs, but the explanatory power is not particularly strong.

The second explanation places less emphasis on the income elasticity of demand for services, but argues that demand for services may increase for two important exogenous reasons. Because of significant changes in the structure of family life—most notably the rapidly increasing female labour force participation rate—personal services, once provided within the household, are now being provided by outside specialist firms. Obvious examples include day care, restaurants and housekeeping services. Thus, these services, which were previously not measured because the transaction took place outside of the market mechanism, are now being recorded because they are taking place at arm's length. An equivalent, and statistically more important, argument can be made for services to business firms. With changes in the structure of business organization made possible by technological change, many business services, once produced within the firm, have increasingly been "contracted-out" to independent service producers. Management consulting, data processing, accounting, financial and legal services are important examples of services whose output, price and input characteristics are now being measured because they too are being provided through arm's length transactions within a market mechanism. Previously, when these business services were being provided by "in-house" production, there was no statistical record kept of the volume of transactions.

Empirical testing of this second explanation has relied almost exclusively on input-output methodology. An early study by Fuchs (1968) in the United States, and more recent work by the Economic

Council (1978) and Magun (1982) in Canada, find little statistical evidence to support the contention. For example, Magun (1982) shows that service sector inputs as a percentage of total inputs absorbed by the goods sector of the Canadian economy increased only from 20.9 percent in 1969 to 21.9 percent in 1979. Because input-output statistics are collected at the establishment level of the producing organization, questions regarding the robustness of this research methodology remain. For example, when input-output data are collected at the establishment level, it is often difficult to distinguish between service inputs which are external to the establishment, but internal to the company or enterprise level of organization. These intra-firm transfers of service inputs are extremely difficult to measure accurately, and may account for the low explanatory power assigned to the contracting-out explanation.

The final, and statistically most important explanation for the growing relative importance of service sector output and employment levels, is based on the observation of a differential rate of labour productivity growth in the service and manufacturing sectors. Specifically, it is believed that labour productivity has grown more slowly in the service sector in comparison to the manufacturing and primary sectors. This difference is thought to be a result of difficulties in standardizing the production of many service outputs without significant loss in product quality, and the perceived lower rate of technological advance in the service sector. With slower than average productivity growth in the service sector, average service production costs and output prices will rise relative to the manufacturing sector. Given the statistical observation that the price elasticity of service demand is less than unity, the higher than average service sector price increase implies that the service sector share of total employment will increase as the economy expands. Despite the problems associated with measuring service outputs and prices, the lagging service sector productivity explanation appears to be the most empirically sound.

In three related articles separated by many years, William Baumol (1967, 1985a and 1985b) expands on this theme of differential productivity growth by developing a simple, two-sector growth model. The earlier version of this model divided the economy into a "stagnant" service sector, which is assumed to have a very low rate of productivity growth, and a "progressive" manufacturing sector with a more rapid rate of productivity advancement. Although the author readily admits that this simple allocation of industries into only two productivity classes is a gross oversimplification, it is, nevertheless, an acceptable starting point from which several interesting results emerge. First, with the passage of time, it is concluded that unit costs in the stagnant service sector, relative to the manufacturing sector, will rise without limit. This phenomenon, dubbed the "cost disease" of the service sector, rests on the simple observation that the low productivity service sector requires relatively more and more input quantities (mainly labour) per unit of output as time passes. Second, if the output proportions of the two sectors remain fairly constant, and if relative prices correspond to relative costs over time, then it can be shown that the share of national expenditure targeted on the stagnant service outputs must rise with the passage of time. Finally, the net result of this unbalanced pattern of input allocation and expenditure patterns is to reduce the country's overall rate of productivity growth.

Baumol's more recent papers recognize the basic heterogeneity of service sector production technologies to argue that the unitary designation of services as stagnant in terms of productivity growth is too strong. Many service sector outputs—for example, communications and computer technologies—have an underlying production technology which will accommodate technological change and productivity growth. In order to capture the differences in service sector production technologies, Baumol classifies industries into three broad categories. The first category of "stagnant personal services" contains services such as teaching, live artistic performance and medical care. The distinguishing feature of these services is that the quality of the output depends upon the amount of time expended by the supplier. Better education or medical care is obtained when the teacher or doctor supplies more labour time to the transaction, i.e., quality is highly correlated with labour time expended. Services in this category also have the characteristic that standardized, production line types of supply are difficult to introduce due to the need for direct contact between the consumers and producers.

At the other end of the productivity spectrum, Baumol identifies several examples of what are classified as "progressive impersonal services." These services involve almost no contact between users and the labour input involved in the production process. As a result, technological advances have enabled producers to operate with rapidly falling real production costs. In the communications industry, important technological developments in the areas of microwave, coaxial cable and satellite technologies have resulted in significant productivity increases.

The third category of services have been dubbed "asymptotically stagnant impersonal services" by Baumol. These middle productivity service sectors use inputs from both the progressive and stagnant service sectors in fixed proportions. Examples include the data processing industry, which combines computer hardware from the progressive sector with software from the stagnant sector, and television and radio broadcasting which requires one hour of the progressive input of electronic transmission to be combined with one hour of program production, the stagnant input. The awkward name given to service industries in this class actually has been chosen with a purpose because of an important behavioral characteristic which causes activities in this sector to eventually behave like services in the stagnant personal service sector. When the service output is produced by combining inputs from both high and low productivity sectors, the overall rate of productivity advance is a weighted average of the two, where the weights are the percentage shares of total input costs. However, if one input has a dramatic rate of per unit cost decrease caused by large productivity gains, while the other has constant or increasing costs, the cost weights used will shift in favour of the zero productivity sector over time. Eventually, as the relative importance, in terms of input cost share, of the progressive service inputs falls, the overall rate of productivity increase is dominated by the stagnant sector input. Baumol (1985a, p. 304) notes that,

> "if 80% of a cost figure declines at an annual rate of 25% compounded, while the other 20% component rises at a rate of 6%, a reversal in the proportion of the two cost components requires just about 20 years"

Thus, the productivity history of services in this category is at first extremely good, and sometimes spectacular, as the declining cost service input dominates the overall input cost configuration. Unfortunately, the seeds for an asymptotic approach to the productivity growth of the stagnant personal service sector are embedded in the simple arithmetic of input cost shares.

Baumol argues that the data processing industry is the best example of an asymptotically stagnant sector, although television and radio broadcasting, and research and development activities are other important examples. In the computation industry, the cost per unit of computation has declined dramatically due to the rapidly falling costs of computer hardware, and despite the more slowly rising costs of labour required for software production. However, as hardware costs fall, they become a smaller and smaller proportion of the total cost of computation, and eventually are outweighed by the rising costs of labour intensive software development. The dramatic decline in aggregate computational costs which have dominated this industry during its early years, must soon come to an end, and unit costs will rise in a parallel fashion to the software costs.

The implications of this three sector categorization of the service sector are brought out empirically by using four separate measures of productivity for 14 sectors of the US economy. When industries are ranked in terms of productivity growth, and allocated to one of the three productivity categories, several conclusions of the model are supported by the data. For the purpose of this summary, two of the conclusions are most important. First, the so-called "cost disease" prediction that relative to the progressive sector, the price of outputs produced in stagnant sectors will rise at a rate equal to the difference in productivity growth is confirmed. Second, the hypothesized rising share of employment in the stagnant sectors is strongly supported using four different measures of employment.

Finally, Robert Inman (1985) combines insights from Fuchs's early work, and Baumol's general equilibrium work on differential rates of productivity growth, to produce a reduced form equation which governs the relative growth in the share of service sector employment over time. By assuming reasonable values for the various parameters in the equation, Inman concludes that the lower rate of productivity growth in the service sector accounts for 55 percent of the annual rate of change of service sector employment. This rising income hypothesis accounts for only 14 percent of the annual change, while the exogenous explanations of contracting-out household and business services explains the remaining 31 percent.

3.4 Services in Regional Development: The General Equilibrium Approach

In its 1984 report entitled *Western Transition*, the Economic Council of Canada introduced the concept that productivity growth and unexploited agglomeration economies in the service industries can generate significant economic growth in Western Canada. In fact, the Council puts enough emphasis on this concept of service led growth that they argue services may conceivably substitute for growth forces which traditionally have come from the natural resource base. Swan (1985) presents a simple partial equilibrium model of the hypothesis that services can be an engine of regional growth, and that the effects will be more important for the western provinces than elsewhere because they will substantially mitigate the effects of the resource production slowdown. McRae (1985) and Mansell (1985) were both critical of the Council's position for a variety of conceptual and empirical reasons but mainly because no well documented, regional general equilibrium model is presented to support the policy conclusions reached. The notion that productivity growth in the service sector will be strong enough to increase regional per capita income levels through linkages with the manufacturing and primary resource sectors is an appealing concept which has fortunately received some recent theoretical attention.

In a recent paper, Melvin (1987) presents a formal general equilibrium model of the role that services could play in a regional economy. Two important dimensions are added to the earlier partial equilibrium work by Swan. First, service industries are modelled in a way that allows them to be traded either interregionally or internationally. This is an important addition which reflects observed behaviour and allows for the possibility that service exports can be an important source of regional income. The second addition is to break out of the confines of a partial equilibrium analysis, and allow for a full trading general equilibrium modelling of the issue. Melvin then uses this model to define whether or not a productivity enhancement in service sector production increases regional welfare, i.e., serve as an engine of growth, and what effect the change may have on output levels, commodity prices and the distribution of income within the region or country.

With Swan's rather simple definition that an engine of growth is defined to be ". . . any change in economic conditions that contributes to raising per capita living standards in that year", Melvin shows that technological improvement in either the goods or services sectors could be classified as an engine of growth. For the simplest case of a small trading region producing and consuming a single service commodity and a single manufactured good, a technological improvement in service production unambiguously makes residents of the region better off in terms of attainable consumption levels. The resulting distribution of income between capital and labour after the technological change will have one factor worse off in real terms and the other factor better off. Which factor wins and which loses depends on the factor intensities assumed for the two industries.

When the simplifying small region assumption is removed, however, there is no longer any presumption that technological progress in the service industry will unambiguously increase average per capita income levels. If the trading region is engaged in trade with other regions each of whom is assumed to be large enough to affect the new equilibrium commodity prices, i.e., terms-of-trade, after the technological improvement, the link between improved technology and increased per capita income levels breaks down. Depending on the region in which the technological improvement takes place, and the assumed capital intensity of the two sectors, it is possible for technological change to increase or decrease per capita income levels. Also, the effects on factor income distribution are indeterminate. The difference between this specification and the previous one is that movement in the terms-of-trade against the home region may be strong enough to offset the initial efficiency-enhancing movements due to technological improvement. Melvin concludes that no general conclusions can be reached concerning the welfare effects, nor the regional income distribution consequences, when technological change takes place in the service sector. The argument that service industries can serve as an engine of regional economic growth may hold in some circumstances, but it is not an unambiguously valid observation. Such a conclusion depends upon whether the region is small, and the specific commodity in which the region has a comparative advantage, i.e., the regional trade pattern. The effects of technological change on regional income distribution depends on the trade pattern and whether the service industry is capital or labour intensive.

Melvin's analysis is one of the few attempts to explicitly model services and regional economic growth, in a general equilibrium context, but empirical testing of his conjectures has proven to be a difficult task. A step in the direction of empirical testing was taken by

Norrie and Percy (1988) in their work on regional general equilibrium models, but it must be stressed that their modelling efforts, while relevant to this focus on service industries, was actually developed for different purposes. Their primary focus was to better understand the process by which a small, resource rich regional economy adjusts to an exogenous change in its terms-of-trade, or changes in the availability of factors of production. Service industries figure prominently in the adjustment story, but the precise specifications adopted by the authors are driven by the need to model interregional adjustment, and less by the need to understand service industries' roles specifically.

Several issues are worth noting. First, Norrie and Percy typically require only two service sectors in their regional modelling efforts. The simple distinction between traded and non-traded services is sufficient for their purposes, but a more detailed look at the service sector's role in regional economic development would require a distinction between personal, business, government and non-profit activities at the least. A second issue is that the author's adopt a comparative statics methodology in which the object is to understand the difference between pre-and post-shock equilibria. As such, the models developed have nothing to say about the equilibrium pattern of income differentials, i.e., they are solved in a "rate-of-change" as opposed to a "levels" format. This follows because the primary purpose has been to document the adjustment process to exogenous shocks. The third issue concerns the availability of data on the regional trade pattern of service outputs. Put bluntly, the existing interregional service sector data do not allow believable simulations of the adjustment to shocks originating in the service sector. Only a rough idea exists concerning which services are interregionally tradeable and which are not, and the data on service flows obtained from the 1974 and 1979 interregional input-output tables are simply made up. See Norrie and Percy in the volume by McRae and Desbois (1988) for a discussion of this issue. Thus, it is simply not possible to use real interregional input-output data to investigate actual links between goods and services trade.

The central analytical issue in the literature on interregional adjustment is easily appreciated. Exchange rates play a key role in theories of adjustment of national economies, and factor mobility typically plays little or none. A regional economy, however, by definition lacks its own exchange rate, and normally has no control over inflows or outflows of capital and labour. Yet a region like a nation cannot maintain expenditures in excess of production (or the reverse) indefinitely, at least not in the absence of offsetting financial transfers. Thus, the general question is as follows: if currency values cannot fluctuate, but regional factor supplies can vary freely, how does adjustment actually proceed? The specific question of importance to this monograph concerns the role played by service industries in this process, and whether or not this function depends in any way on the size or rate of growth of such activities?

Without getting involved in the technical details of model construction, there are some general results from the work of Norrie and Percy which are of interest to the question of service industries in regional economic development. Attention will focus on the range of possible outcomes, and the process of regional adjustment to exogenous changes in terms-of-trade, or changes in the availability of factors of production.

The adjustment scenarios predicted by Norrie and Percy's regional, general equilibrium model depend on three issues—the time frame assumed for the adjustment process; the specification of the labour market adopted; and whether or not "add-on" details such as agglomeration economies and government spending/taxation are included. Within each scenario, the specific results depend on the values of the various important parameters embedded within the model. Results may be briefly discussed under the categories short run, flexible wage; short run, sticky wage; long run; agglomeration economies; and government spending/taxation.

3.4.1 *Short Run - Flexible Wage*

Short run scenarios assume that factor supplies to the region are fixed, although labour can be reallocated across sectors within the economy. This is the scenario where the nominal wage rate acts most obviously as an exchange rate to bring about adjustment. An improvement in the regional terms of trade—the shock assumed to have taken place— increases real income, and hence, spending within the region (the income effect) and draws factors to the booming resource sector (the resource movement effect). The resultant excess demand for labour drives up the nominal wage rate. Non-booming export sectors and import competing ones see their output levels decline as a result. They cannot pass on increased costs due to the assumed high price elasticities of demand for their products. The same consequence is true for tradeable services. Non-tradeable services can pass on higher costs, so the net impact on their output levels is uncertain—the ultimate result depends on a host of price, income and substitution elasticities. One can effectively generate any outcome, depending on what values are assigned to these parameters. The income distribution consequences follow directly. Labour income rises, as does that of specific factors of production in expanding sectors. Specific factors in declining sectors lose. The model works in reverse for declines in the terms of trade.

3.4.2 *Short Run - Sticky Wage*

If wages are modelled to be sticky in either direction, the main adjustment takes place in employment levels. Labour is drawn out of unemployment, meaning that the spillover effects on other sectors are minimized. This formulation is effectively equivalent to postulating a perfectly elastic supply of labour over some range. If the output effects on other sectors are muted, so too are income redistribution trends. Sticky wages also mean less induced diversification if the leading sector slumps. Labour is released into unemployment rather than putting downward pressure on wages, and hence, costs in other export and import competing industries.

3.4.3 *The Long Run*

Capital and labour can move into or out of the region in the longer run, and supplies of land and natural resources can be developed. Factor mobility thus becomes the main avenue of adjustment in these scenarios. If supplies of capital and labour are perfectly elastic, then all of the stories based on resource movement effects are undone in the longer run. Real wages will return to their initial equilibrium value, as will nominal rental rates on capital. The size of the economy alone will change to satisfy the equilibrium conditions. Returns to specific factors can still vary, however, so there can be income distributional effects. If factor supply elasticities are finite, the short run adjustment is only partially undone. The new equilibrium will lie somewhere between that for the short run and that for the long run, assuming perfectly elastic factor responses.

The concept of long run equilibrium for a regional economy is further complicated by the fact that it is difficult to decide exactly what is an appropriate assumption to make regarding balance of payments equilibrium. Regional absorption can exceed production as long as financial transfers are available, and vice versa for capital exporting regions. Otherwise, some ultimate equilibrating mechanism must come into play—essentially some variant of the old gold standard literature given the existence of fixed exchange rates across regions. Experimentation with this requirement has shown that the simulation results are quite sensitive.

Welfare judgements are also much more difficult to make in the longer run as well, since the regional population has changed. Does one consider original residents only, or newcomers as well? If there has been outmigration, do we consider the welfare of original residents now living elsewhere? The problem is quite serious because conclusions can be reversed by choosing a different definition of the regional population.

3.4.4 *Agglomeration Economies*

The simulations have experimented with a formulation modelling agglomeration economies as a form of technological change.[1] The endogeneity comes from making unit costs in manufacturing and services decline steadily as population increases. In these scenarios, an improvement in the terms-of-trade effect draws population to the region, which reduces unit costs in the affected sectors, which tends to offset the crowding out that would otherwise occur due to nominal wage increases. The burden is thus borne by traded sectors not experiencing agglomeration economies—non-booming resource sectors for instance. Technical change also increases real income in the region as well, so this effect must be factored into the final conclusions on resource allocation.

Agglomeration economies are a wild card in models of this type. If the efficiency gains are set large enough, they can reduce costs for a price taking region so much as to lower its terms-of-trade, thus reducing real incomes in the process. Results with models of this type can be so unstable that conclusions drawn from them should be down played. As a policy issue, we need to know much more about agglomeration economies, analytically and empirically, before they can be included confidently in the simulation models.

3.4.5 *Government Spending/Taxation*

This is one of the more interesting features of the simulations produced by Norrie and Percy. Most of the discussion has focussed on the efficiency of government as a rent collector from the primary resource sectors, and, in these models, attention is drawn to the effects that governments can have when spending windfall gains. There are three types of distortions which may be produced by this activity. Lower tax burdens lead to fiscally induced migration, with the attendant costs that that literature discusses. Secondly, explicit subsidies may also act like effective protection measures, distorting the allocation of resources across private sectors. Small economies tend to bear the costs of such actions, since they cannot easily pass them off through terms-of-trade effects. Finally, there is a distortion between the private and the public sectors. Government will tend to spend more from revenues that are not obviously drawn from taxes on personal incomes.

3.4.6 *Summary of General Equilibrium Models*

In summary, the importance of service industries to the process of regional growth has recently undergone a significant transformation. The traditional view is that service industries are thought to be secondary to the primary exporting sectors with demand for local services being supported by means of income generated in the exporting sectors. More recent writers such as North (1955, 1956) and Tiebout (1956) have argued that services may have a more fundamental role in the regional development process by providing the essential framework for the development of export industries. This new optimism for selective service industries reached a peak with the work of Swan (1985) and the Economic Council of Canada (1984). In these publications, the concept that productivity growth and agglomeration economies in service industries can generate significant regional growth—enough to offset the decline expected in the primary resource sectors—was given centre stage. Rigorous regional general equilibrium theorizing provided by Melvin (1987) and Norrie and Percy (1988) show that the relationship between service industries and regional economic growth is a good deal more complicated than presented by Swan and the Economic Council. Unfortunately, two empirical issues need to be resolved before regional general equilibrium models can be used to investigate the relationship between regional economic performance and service sector growth. First, researchers need to distinguish between traded and non-traded services. Changes in transportation and communications technology combined with regulatory changes allowing for greater market access have expanded the boundaries of traded services. Some evidence is available from questionnaire surveys—this is the subject of the next section—but no systematic data base on traded service industries currently exists. The lack of actual data on interregional flows of service outputs is the second empirical problem. Information from the 1974 and 1979 interregional input-output tables would seem to be applicable, but Norrie's essay in McRae and Desbois (1988) shows that these service flow data are not appropriate.

3.5 Services in Regional Development: Other Approaches

Regional economists and economic geographers have developed a variety on non-general equilibrium models which have been, or may be, applied to help explain the spatial pattern of services industries. Three models or theories stand out.

- The regional life cycle model is based on the premise that as a service moves through various stages of its product life cycle, it generates changing locational requirements. Only when the service production technology reaches the "standardized" production stage does it become truly "footloose", and decentralization occurs on a larger scale. At this point, service producing firms seek out low-cost, peripheral regions where production costs, and especially labour costs, are lower. At the international level, the mechanism by which the standardized service production technology is transferred to a lower cost location often involves multinational enterprises.

- Diffusion theory stresses the role of technological change in determining patterns of regional economic development. The various levels of service sector development in the country are thought to reflect patterns of adoption or diffusion of technological innovations which are relevant to the service sector.
- The export base approach places primary emphasis on the role of service sector exports as the stimulus to regional growth. Exports of both goods and traded services provide the net injection of income which multiplies throughout the community or region to support region-serving activities. Eventually as this process occurs and region-serving activities proliferate, self-sustaining regional growth begins as agglomeration economies come into play.

It is the third explanation of export base theory which has been most often used in connection with the role of service industries in regional economic growth. In order to understand the notion of export base theory better, it is helpful to make a brief comparison between the partial equilibrium concept of export base, and the general equilibrium models which were the subject of the previous section.

For general equilibrium models, nations or regions are assumed to be in a trading equilibrium where the pattern of trade, i.e., which region exports which commodity, is based upon the principle of comparative advantage. The source of a nation's comparative advantage is based on any of a number of structural factors, but the most common ones are relative abundance of one or more factors of production which are heavily used by one of the domestic industries, or the simple observation that one nation has a technological production advantage over the others for one or more industries. In either case— relative factor abundance or technological advantage—the favoured industry in the favoured country has a relative cost advantage which allows it to export. Offsetting the export sectors are comparative disadvantage sectors which are subjected to import competition. In these traditional trade models, it is not exports *per se* which are an engine of economic growth, but the fact that a previously closed domestic economy is exposed to international competition. Once the required adjustments have taken place to the comparative advantage and disadvantage sectors, both total world and individual country per capita real income can be shown to have increased over the no-trade situation. The important point for this monograph is that export and import competing sectors rise up naturally based on underlying comparative advantages and disadvantages. Import competition *and* exports are both important because they allow for an efficiency enhancing reallocation of production and consumption patters on a world scale.

For economic base models, less attention is paid to the cosmopolitan notion of world and country per capita income, and more is paid to subnational levels of these variables. Now the identification and promotion of export sectors, or import substitutes, takes centre stage because these activities contribute to the creation of an "export surplus" which accrues to one or all of the local factors of production. It is the creation and enhancement of the export surplus which allows employment and income levels to be higher than can be supported by local consumption. In this sense, a sector—either service or goods producing—can be thought of as an engine to local economic growth.

Within the tradition of economic base models, two streams of thought on the importance of service industries to the process of urban and surrounding hinterland development can be identified. A residual role is assigned to services by studies which build upon theorems developed in the tradition of "central place" theory. This literature argues that within any economic region—usually a city and its surrounding hinterland—a hierarchy of market areas emerges with higher order commodities being produced in and exported from the largest centers, and more common goods being located in the smaller market areas. This literature has mostly ignored the regional question of whether or not higher order locations could also export commodities beyond the central place system in which they are located. Also, the theory was originally developed to explain the location pattern of goods producers, but writers such as Reifler (1976) have argued that services fit into the same hierarchical market pattern. In other words, he recognizes that service commodities are being traded, but suggests that the trade pattern is explained in terms of where the urban area fits into the hierarchical structure. Basing his analysis on a statistical association between U.S. service earnings per capita and urban size—not service trade data—Reifler concludes that service commodities are exported from large metropolitan centres and sold to buyers located in smaller centres within the same region. With the conclusion that services are basically localized in nature—flowing from higher to lower order centres within the same region—Reifler argues that service industries may respond to, but cannot initiate, regional growth and development, and hence, are not suitable as a foundation for regional development efforts. In this analysis the service sector is viewed as a residual category of non-productive, population serving activities whose nature and distribution are determined by the size, standard of living and distribution of the population and extent of goods production.

A second and somewhat more recent analysis of the role of service industries uses the conceptual framework of economic base theory more directly and notes that many service outputs can be traded interregionally or internationally. According to this conceptual framework, the economic base of city or small region has two principal elements—"basic" or export-oriented activities, and "non-basic" or residentiary activities which serve the local population. It is the basic sectors which serve a propulsive function in that they create net fiscal injections into the local economy which stimulate other local economic activity through the multiplier process. Economic base theory has traditionally regarded the principal basic activity or propulsive force of a local economy to be manufacturing. Residentiary activities are induced, non-export oriented and are regarded to be a function of the size of the local population and the dynamism of the local economy, i.e., residentiary activities do not promote growth, but rather follow it. Traditionally, the residentiary sector has been considered to be composed principally of services. The major contribution of recent writers—see W.B. Beyers and Michael Alvine (1985a) and P.W. Daniels (1985)—is to show that services, and especially the producer services segment, are exportable to buyers located outside of the local economy. Thus, it follows that some services in some regions have the potential for stimulating local economic growth. Combining this observation with the information that producer services play a significant role in attracting capital investment and, in some cases, producing and diffusing innovation, it becomes clear that producer services have the *potential* to exert a significant influence upon the spatial pattern of economic development.

The research which flows from this newer view of services in regional development has been mainly empirical, as researchers attempt to document the importance of regionally traded services in large cities or regions, often by means of indirect and proxy measures. The most important analysis of the spatial pattern of service industries in U.S. cities has been done by Noyelle and Stanback (1984). They develop a taxonomy of American cities based on the structure of employment. Their analysis leads to the categorization of four basic types of urban regions:

- "Diversified Advanced Service Centres" are at the pinnacle of the urban hierarchy. Cities in this category have an extensive range of producer services serving a wide variety of service and manufacturing clients. These service sectors collectively make up a significant portion of the local economic base.

- "Specialized Advanced Service Centres" contain urban regions which also have a producer service base, but the service industries are not broadly based, and often suffer the same income fluctuations which are a fundamental feature of regions which are dependent on one or two primary sector outputs.

- "Production Centres" are mainly urban regions which contain manufacturing activities. Producer services are supplied as intra-firm transactions, and as a result, the "stand-alone" producer service sector is relatively underdeveloped.

- "Consumer Oriented Centres" contain urban regions that are mostly residential in nature, thus there is very little scope for producer service industries to grow and prosper.

Noyelle and Stanback use this classification scheme to document the changes in the distribution of U.S. economic activity over the 1959-1976 time period.

The implication of their analysis is that services will not be exported from regions which do not have major metropolitan centres in the upper two categories. Thus the development opportunities for service led growth in regions which lack diversified or specialized service centres are not very good. The increasing importance of service industries combined with the spatial observation that advanced service exports have tended to concentrate in relatively few major cities, produce the conclusion that many areas of the country which lack major metropolitan centres will face enormous developmental problems as the economy shifts toward producing more service outputs.

3.6 Summary

Conceptual work on the role of service industries to the process of regional development has basically divided along research discipline lines. Economists have used the established models of international trade theory by adapting them to a regional format and adding service industries. Both Melvin (1987) and Norrie and Percy (1988) derive prototype regional general equilibrium models based on well established relationships from international trade theory. These regional models in turn build on recent work by Markuson (1987), Jones and Ruane (1987), Burgess (1987) and Ryan (1987). Regional economists and economic geographers have used a number of conceptual models to aid them in better understanding the complex relationships between service industries and regional development. However, for the most part this work is directly or indirectly based on economic base models.

Notes

1. Agglomeration economies are production cost reductions which are achieved by firms when they locate in close proximity of one another. The reasons why cost reductions might occur include: larger markets for local manufacturers; denser and more efficient communications network; increased possibilities for specialization among firms; economies in the provision of local government services; more sophisticated capital and labour markets etc.

Chapter 4

Service Industries, Regional and Urban Development: Some Empirical Results

4.1 Introduction

In addition to the conceptual problems involving service industries and regional economic development, the lack of actual data on inter-regional flows of service outputs effectively precludes the empirical testing of regional general equilibrium models involving service industries. Norrie, in McRae and Desbois (1988, p.217), shows that the service estimates contained in Statistics Canada's regional input-output tables are of no use in studying connections between tradeable services and regional economic performance. Norrie points out that no serious empirical work on service sector exports and regional economic performance can be done until Statistics Canada is able to provide data on trade in services based on survey techniques.

Given this national lack of service sector trade data, several small surveys have been undertaken by various researchers on an *ad hoc* basis. This chapter will review in detail some recent work done for the City of Vancouver by McRae and Desbois (1987), and compare the results to previous work done for Montreal and Seattle by other researchers.

4.2   The Service Sector in Vancouver: Profile, Problems and Potential

4.2.1   *The Universe of Vancouver Based Service Producing Establishments*

In order to generate a list of service producing establishments from which a representative sample could be obtained, a data base was purchased from a private firm which compiles and records relevant business data on individual business establishments in the Vancouver area. The data base contains information on 43,787 Vancouver and Lower Mainland establishments. Entries are classified by four digit SIC codes, and information is collected on the number of employees, the establishments' organizational structure (sales office, branch office or headquarters) as well as the address, telephone number and name of the chief executive officer.

The choice of sectors to be included in the analysis was restricted to "pure" service producing establishments. While this may seem to be an obvious restriction to place on data to be used for a study of the service sector, it is more important than might be commonly realized. Establishments in other sectors of the local economy—especially manufacturing and primary producers—may also produce and sell service commodities to local affiliates in other regions or countries via intrafirm trade. In fact, Statistics Canada (1988, 67-510) reports that in 1983/84, the manufacturing sector accounted for 30 percent of the international receipts and 40 percent of the international payments for the business services categories. Service transactions conducted as intra-firm transactions through manufacturing or primary product firms have been excluded from the analysis, not because they are likely to be empirically irrelevant, but because they are not the main focus of this exploratory research. From the list of service producing establishments, two additional operational rules helped guide the specific choice of service sectors to be studied. First, it was decided that emphasis should be placed on the category of business services produced and sold by private sector organizations. Thus, services such as education and health, when provided directly by the public sector, have been excluded from the analysis. The second rule which guided the choice of service sectors to be included involves the "vehicle" by which the service is traded interregionally or internationally. Only service establishments whose outputs are capable of being exported directly to final buyers, or indirectly, via contractual or affiliate relationships with non-local firms, have been included. Services such as tourism whose export requires the buyer to physically travel to Vancouver to consume the service have been excluded.

With these two "filters" in place, our choice of included service establishments, at the four-digit SIC code level, represents approximately 220 sectors consisting of 13,175 establishments. Removing sectors for which there were no reported Vancouver area establishments and sectors which experience and previous studies have shown to be entirely local in nature (local and interurban passenger transit and several sub-categories within the real estate group) resulted in a final list of 175 sectors. For purposes of analysis throughout this chapter, the universe of 175 sectors has been grouped into 35 major subgroups, and five major groups, containing 11,822 establishments. The major groups are:[1]

- Services incidental to the primary sector
- Construction
- Transportation and Communications
- Finance, Insurance and Real Estate (FIRE)
- Business Services

Business services are the largest category (55.4 percent), followed by FIRE (20.0 percent), the transportation and communications sector (15.1 percent), services incidental (7.1 percent) and construction (2.4 percent). The construction sector includes all construction services except residential building construction and special trade contractors. The services incidental grouping includes services incidental to agriculture, forestry and mining. The transportation and communications sector excludes local and interurban passenger transit and postal services. Transportation establishments account for 13.1 percent of the entries, while communications and utilities account for the remaining 2 percent. The FIRE sector includes all financial services, except bank and credit agencies,[2] all insurance establishments, and all real estate sectors except apartment building operators, other dwelling operators, mobile home site operators and railroad property leasors. Of the 2,362 establishments identified in this sector, 10 percent are in financial services, 33 percent in insurance and 57 percent in real estate. Finally, the large business services category consists of 6,544 establishments, of whom 83 percent provide direct services to business. The remaining entries are private health services (5.6 percent), leisure services (4.9 percent), private education services (3.9 percent), and other services (2.6 percent).

Figure 4.1 shows the distribution of the universe of establishments by organizational status—branch office, headquarters or single office—and sector. For all five major sectors, the dominant organizational form, for the majority of establishments, is single office. Branch offices of enterprises controlled elsewhere in Canada, or the world, are most important in the transportation and communications sector and, to a lesser extent, the FIRE sector. Head offices average 8 percent of establishments for all sectors combined, and are relatively more important in the construction, services incidental and transportation/communications sectors.

Figure 4.1
Distribution of Establishments
by Organizational Status and Sector

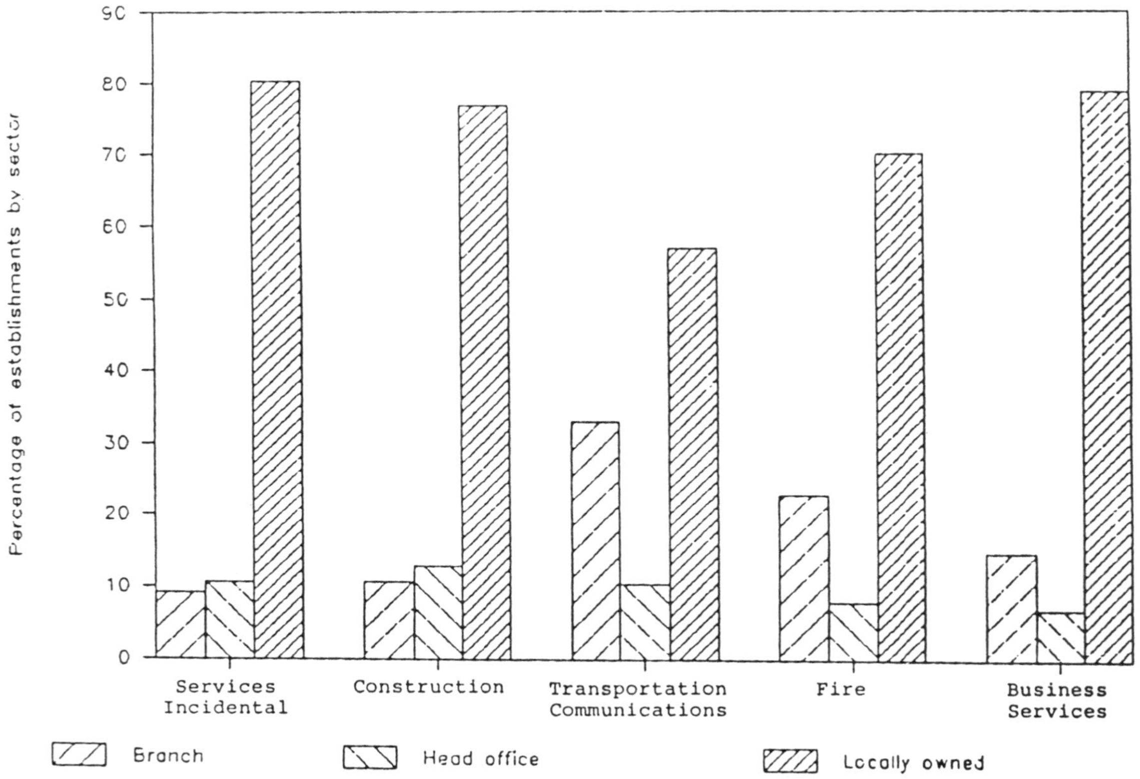
Percentage of establishments by sector
90
80
70
60
50
40
30
20
10
0
Services Incidental
Construction
Transportation Communications
Fire
Business Services
Branch
Head office
Locally owned

Finally, the employment characteristics of the universe of service producing establishments, and the break-out by sector, is shown in Figure 4.2 For all sectors aggregated together, it is apparent that small firms dominate large firms in terms of the number of establishments. For example, 68 percent of the establishments in the universe have fewer than five employees, and 92.8 percent have fewer than 26 employees. In terms of specific sectors, the services incidental to the primary sector has the highest percentage of small establishments as 82 percent of the establishments have five or fewer employees. The transportation/communications and construction sectors have the lowest proportion of small establishments.

Considering the universe data all at once, and focussing on the organizational structure, location, and number of employee issues produces the conclusion that the five major service sector groupings are basically similar in terms of underlying characteristics. The major differences which emerge are restricted to the construction and transportation/communications sectors. These two groups are relatively larger, and at least for the transportation/communications sector, relatively less dominated by single office establishments.

Because the FIRE and business services sectors contain many important subsectors, it is instructive to disaggregate the data universe for these sectors. Table 4.1 shows organizational status, and size information for the FIRE grouping disaggregated into the three component sectors of financial services, insurance and real estate. All subsectors within the FIRE group display the same basic organizational status, but real estate is relatively more dominated by single office establishments, and insurance has more branch offices. In terms of size, as measured by the number of employees, the real estate subsector tends to be more dominated by small establishments.

Table 4.2 shows the same information on organizational status, and size for the disaggregated business sector. Dividing the business service sector into four subsectors does not drastically change the conclusions already obtained because the aggregate data is so dominated by the subcategory of corporate services. However, it may be noted that the health and other services categories are less dominated by single office establishments.

Given the importance of the corporate services sub-category (5,428 establishments), Table 4.3 further disaggregates this group into 20 more finely defined categories. As is readily apparent, there is no one category of activity which dominates the corporate services subcategory. The management and public relations group is the largest, accounting for 16.5 percent of the subcategory. Thus, observations on the corporate services subcategory are based on a reasonable distribution for establishments across the 20 categories of activities, and the corporate services group as a whole easily dominates the business services category.

Figure 4.2
Distribution of Establishments
by Sector and Number of Employees

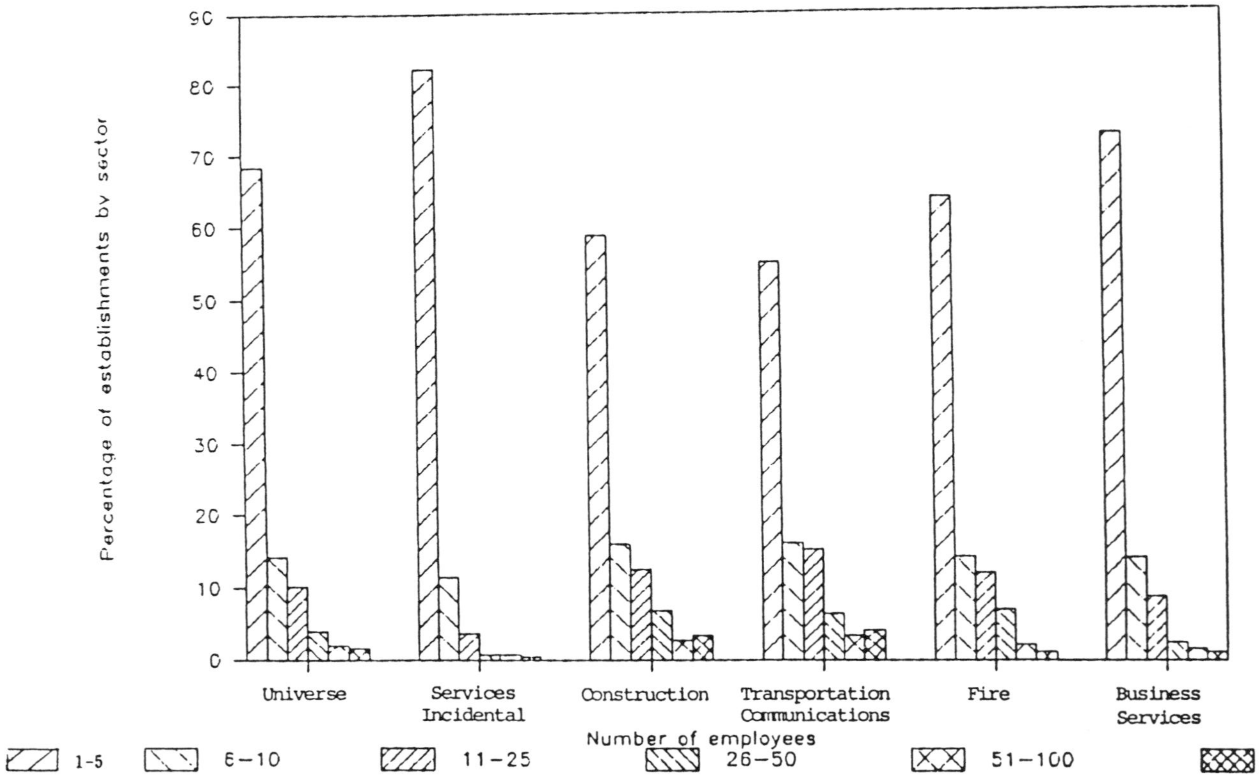

Table 4.1
Percentage Distribution of FIRE Establishments
by Status and Size

Sector	Number of Establishments	Organizational Status		
		Branch (%)	Headquarters (%)	Single Office (%)
Financial Services	230	27.4	12.2	60.4
Insurance	749	36.8	8.1	55.0
Real Estate	1,383	14.7	7.3	82.9

	Size-Number of Employees							
	1-5	6-10	11-25	26-50	51-100	101-250	251-500	500+
Financial Services	61.3	12.2	10.4	8.7	4.8	2.2	0.4	0.0
Insurance	59.7	15.8	14.2	7.1	2.1	1.1	0.0	0.1
Real Estate	69.7	14.3	11.7	7.0	1.5	0.5	0.1	0.2

4.2.2 *The Mail-Out and Questionnaire Samples*

From the universe of service producing establishments, a population was selected by means of disproportional stratified sampling. Specifically, 3 "strata" were created which allowed establishments to be sorted by employee level—1 to 5 employees, 6 to 10 employees and those with 11 or more employees. From these "strata", a random start interval technique was used to select,

- 1 in 20 establishments from the group of small establishments (1-5 employees);
- 1 in 2 establishments from the group of establishments with 6 to 10 employees;

and all establishments in the last strata. This technique generated a population of 3,333 establishments. The population created was used to generate two groups of establishments—one to receive an in-depth personal interview, the other to receive a shorter version, mail-out questionnaire. The group chosen to receive the personal interview consisted of all establishments of 100 or more employees, and a representative group of establishments in terms of service sector, organizational status and employee size. All other establishments in

Table 4.2
Percentage Distribution of Business Service Establishments
by Status and Size

Sector	Number of Establishments	Organizational Status		Single Office (%)
		Branch (%)	Headquarters (%)	
Corporate Services	5,428	11.9	6.8	81.4
Health Services	369	27.6	6.7	65.6
Education Services	257	19.8	7.0	73.2
Leisure Services	321	19.3	5.6	75.1
Other Services	169	51.5	14.8	33.7

	Size-Number of Employees							
	1-5	6-10	11-25	26-50	51-100	101-250	251-500	500+
Corporate Services	72.5	14.0	8.5	2.4	1.5	0.7	0.3	0.0
Health Services	73.4	11.1	10.0	3.0	0.8	1.1	0.0	0.5
Education Services	65.8	17.1	11.3	2.3	2.7	0.4	0.4	0.0
Leisure Services	78.8	11.5	6.2	1.2	1.6	0.3	0.0	0.3
Other Services	62.7	20.1	13.0	3.0	0.6	0.6	0.0	0.0

the population were mailed a shorter questionnaire and an explanatory cover letter. The interviews took place between July 15, and September 30, 1986. The mail-out questionnaire was mailed on August 8, 1986, and replies were returned, over the following four or five weeks.

Table 4.3
Distribution of Corporate Services

Sector	Number of Establishments	Percentage of Total
Advertising	183	3.4
Credit Reporting & Collection	39	0.7
Commercial Photography	166	3.1
Stenographic & Reproduction NEC	66	1.2
Building Maintenance	265	4.9
News Syndicates	8	0.1
Employment Agencies	81	1.5
Computer Programming, etc.	395	7.3
Research & Development	71	1.3
Management & Public Relations	898	16.5
Detective/Protective Services	71	1.3
Equipment Rental	164	3.0
Photo Finishing Labs	65	1.2
Commercial Testing Labs	19	0.4
Corporate Services NEC	798	14.7
Engineering/Architecture	697	12.8
Non Commercial Research	19	0.4
Accounting/Auditing	610	11.2
Miscellaneous Services NEC	60	1.1
Lawyer	753	13.9
TOTAL	5,428	100.0

For the interview questionnaire, 450 establishments were identified as potential interviewees. During the course of the interview period, 428 of the establishments were contacted by phone, and a sample interview questionnaire and explanatory letter sent out. This procedure resulted in 168 completed interviews by September 30, and 260 non-participants. From the set of non-participants, the largest group (57 percent) was not interested in providing data on the establishment's operation, or the person contacted did not have time to participate. Another 22 percent of the establishments were no longer in operation, or had moved leaving no forwarding address. Several establishments (13 percent) would not participate because they did not feel they produced service outputs. The remaining 8 percent of the non-respondents gave no reason for their refusal to participate. Removing the establishments who were no longer in operation or could not be located, and the ones who were not service producers, leaves an overall net response rate of 60 percent to the request for an interview.

After manually removing duplicate listings from the remaining 2,883 establishments in the population (3,333 - 450), the net result for the mail-out questionnaire was 2,863 establishments. All received a personal letter explaining the purpose of the project, a short questionnaire and an addressed, stamped return envelope. At the end of the data collection phase, 330 questionnaires were completed and returned in sufficient detail to be usable. We received 53 responses from establishments either refusing to participate, or not eligible because they did not consider themselves to produce a service output. A further 142 questionnaires were returned because of an incorrect or incomplete address. Over half of these (79) were re-addressed and mailed again. Removing the 53 refusals, and the 63 (142 - 79) questionnaires which were incorrectly addressed, produced a net response rate of 12.0 percent. The response from the mail survey was quite low, but not unexpected given other response rates for similar mail survey efforts. Statistical details on non-respondents are provided in Appendix B.

4.2.3 *Results of the Survey*

For ease of analysis and ultimate policy discussion, the results obtained from the survey of service producing establishments are arranged under the following headings:

- type of customers;
- the extent to which services are exported interregionally or internationally;
- the age of service producing establishments;
- the factors which influenced establishments to locate in the Greater Vancouver area;
- the reasons and mechanisms by which the sample establishments entered export markets;
- the extent and importance of interprovincial and international barriers to market access.

As noted in Chapter 3, the traditional view of service outputs is that they are "residentiary" in nature, i.e., they are sold directly to local individuals or households as personal services, or to the manufacturing sector and embodied in the physical good for export to other regions and countries. The linkage of service sector sales to the manufacturing sector is an important one because it provides the conceptual basis for public sector support of the manufacturing sector. In other words, if manufacturing establishments can be induced to expand, modernize and export through public programs, the service sector will share in the benefits through their input ties to manufacturing. Services are not thought to be a suitable base for regional development support because, in this view, they are only population-serving, and thus their existence and size is merely a function of the size and per capita income level of the local population. In order to investigate this issue empirically, both the mail-out and interview questionnaires asked respondents to allocate their gross service revenue by class of customer:

- household/individual;
- business establishments in the agricultural/natural resource or manufacturing sectors;
- business establishments in the service sector;
- government, including Crown corporations.

The results of this exercise, for both the interview and mail-out questionnaires are displayed in Table 4.4. This table shows that 48.9 percent of the establishments who responded to this question on the mail-out questionnaire report that they earned no revenue at all from the direct sale of their services to households or individuals. The corresponding number for the interview was even higher (61.5 percent). Both samples support the hypothesis that sales of services directly to households or individuals are relatively unimportant, as 68.7 percent of the mail-out questionnaire respondents and 80.1 percent of interviewees report that they earn less than one-quarter of their gross service revenue from direct sales to households or individuals.

Equally surprising is the observation that the demand side linkages to British Columbia's primary/manufacturing sector firms are also extremely weak. Table 4.4 shows that 41.6 percent of the mail-out respondents and 60.8 percent of the interviewees report that they sell no services to firms in these sectors. The evidence of low linkages between services and the primary/manufacturing sectors is even stronger when it is realized that service establishments who do sell output to firms in these sectors, typically do not earn much of their gross revenue from this source.

Sales of services to the public sector—either directly to government or to crown corporations—earn no revenue for approximately one-half of the establishments in both samples, and earn less than 25 percent of the gross service revenue for an additional 31 percent of the sample establishments. Like the household/individual and primary/manufacturing sectors, sales of services to the public sector are not overwhelmingly important.

The data contained in Table 4.4 will, however, support the contention that the major market for Vancouver-based service producing establishments is other service sector firms. Both survey instruments

Table 4.4
Percentage Distribution of Sample Establishments Revenue
by Quartile by Customer

	Mail Questionnaire Sample (%)				Interview Questionnaire Sample (%)			
	Hsehold/ Indiv. (n=313)	Primary/ Manuf. (n=310)	Service Sector (n=310)	Gov't (n=311)	Hsehold/ Indiv. (n=102)	Primary/ Manuf. (n=154)	Service Sector (n=154)	Gov't (n=118)
% of Total Gross Service Revenue								
0	48.9	41.6	17.7	49.8	61.5	60.8	26.6	49.4
1-24	19.8	33.9	19.0	30.5	18.6	39.2	20.8	30.5
25-49	7.0	10.3	16.5	7.1	3.2	0.0	13.0	4.5
50-74	7.7	6.1	18.1	6.8	6.4	0.0	16.9	4.5
75-100	16.6	8.0	28.7	5.8	10.3	0.0	22.7	11.0

show a very low percentage of service establishments—17.7 percent for the mail-out questionnaire and 26.6 percent for the interview—who earn no revenue selling outputs to other service sector firms. The remainder earn some proportion of their gross revenue selling outputs to the other service sector establishments, and many—28.7 percent of the mail-out questionnaire establishments and 22.7 percent of the interview establishments—are tightly linked in that they earn between 75 percent and 100 percent of their gross revenue from sales to other service sector firms. The concept of services as closely tied to demands originating in the individual/household or manufacturing sectors is not supported by these data.

The Economic Council of Canada (1984), using employment data from the OECD countries, reach a similar conclusion, that the growth of service outputs seems to be more closely tied to intraservice sector demands, than to the manufacturing sector. They observe (p. 157) that,

"The number of workers increased in manufacturing throughout the 1950's and 1960's in all of these (the OECD) countries. Between 1971 and 1981, however, the number of manufacturing workers actually declines in the United

Kingdom, France and West Germany. Indeed, the fastest rate of decrease in the number of manufacturing workers occurred in the United Kingdom and West Germany, which had the largest proportion of workers in manufacturing throughout the period. Therefore, essentially all of the new jobs created in these European countries were in the service sector. This suggests that the observed job growth in services cannot be dependent on job growth in the goods-producing industries, for there was no such growth. It could still be argued, however, on the basis of this evidence alone, that growth in services was dependent on output growth in the goods industry. That seems to us unlikely, . . ."

When these data on type of clients are disaggregated by sector, some interesting differences are noted, but it must be remembered that the number of observations—especially for the interview sample—is significantly reduced. For clarity of presentation, only the conclusions are presented in this section. The tables from which the conclusions are drawn are available in McRae and Desbois (1987). For establishments in the FIRE sector, both the mail-out and interview samples confirm that the majority of clients are in the household/individual or service sectors. Compared to the transportation/communications and business service sectors, establishments in the FIRE sector derive the highest proportion of revenue from sales to final consumers. For example, 52 percent of the FIRE establishments in the mail-out sample, and 58 percent in the questionnaire sample, earn more than one-half of their gross service revenue from sales to households or individuals. Also, when the results are compared to the pooled data of Table 4.4, it appears that establishments in the FIRE sector have the lowest proportion of sales to the public sector. Seventy-two percent of the FIRE establishments in the mail-out sample, and nearly 70 percent in the interview sample, report that they earn no revenue from sales to the public sector.

In the transportation/communications sector, the pattern of sales is basically similar to that identified by pooled sample data, except for the fact that sales to firms in the primary/manufacturing sectors are considerably more important for transportation/communications establishments. Thus, the main class of customers for establishments in this sector are sales to other service sector firms, or sales to firms located in the primary/manufacturing sectors. Sales to both households/individuals, or to government remain relatively unimportant.

In terms of demand side linkages, establishments in the business services category are firmly tied to other service sector establishments through a system of intraservices sector demands. Also, the business service category is, in comparison to the FIRE and transportation/communication sectors, more closely linked to the public sector through sales to government and Crown corporations. Revenue earned from sales of business services to the households/individual and primary/manufacturing sectors remain relatively unimportant.

In summary, the conclusions on type of clients drawn from the aggregated data of Table 4.4 mask some interesting differences between the sectors. The overall importance of the service sector as a source of demand for the output of our sample of service producing establishments is due to the observation that all three subcategories earn a significant proportion of their revenue selling outputs to other service sector firms. It is this observation—valid for FIRE, transportation/communications and business service establishments— which supports the observation that the growth of the service sector overall is not directly linked to demands originating in the household/individual, primary/manufacturing or public sectors of the economy. However, each of the three subsectors which collectively make up both the mail-out and interview samples also has an important demand side link to one of these other client classes in addition to the service sector. For example, service establishments in the FIRE category earn a significant portion of their revenues selling output to households and individuals; establishments in the transportation/communications grouping sell to the primary/manufacturing sector; and business service establishments also sell to the public sector in addition to their sales to other service sector firms. The net result, when these sectoral data are pooled, is that the service sector is the most important source of demand for the output of service establishments, but each of the three subsectors has an important additional link to one of remaining classes of demanders. This latter observation can be overlooked when dealing only with pooled data.

Finally, both questionnaires asked respondents to identify the proportion of their gross service revenues which were earned by intraorganizational sales. Seventy-five percent of the establishments answering the mail-out questionnaire, and 71.2 percent of the personal interview respondents, reported that they earn no revenue from sales to linked or affiliated companies, i.e., the vast majority of their revenue comes from "arms-length" sales. Even when establishments report some intraorganizational revenue, it typically accounts for less than one-quarter of the gross service revenue. Disaggregating by service sector into its three component categories did not significantly change this conclusion.

The revenue earned by respondents to both the mail-out and interview questionnaires was allocated into six different categories of export business:

- Establishment revenue earned on business exclusively in Greater Vancouver.
- Establishment revenue earned on business exclusively in British Columbia (includes establishments doing business

both in Greater Vancouver and somewhere else in the province).

- Establishment revenue earned on business exclusively in Canada (includes establishments doing business both in B.C. and elsewhere in Canada).

- Establishment revenue earned by exporting exclusively to the U.S. (includes establishments doing business both in Canada and the U.S.).

- Establishment revenue earned by exporting both to the U.S. and to the rest of the world (includes establishments doing business both in Canada and outside).

The results are displayed in Table 4.5. For the FIRE sector between 62 percent and 76 percent of the total revenue earned by the sample establishments is generated by local sales, i.e., sales to customers located within Greater Vancouver. The mail questionnaire produced the highest estimate of purely local business for this sector probably due to the fact that establishments in this sample are smaller than for the interview sample. For establishments in the mail questionnaire sample, 24 percent of the total sample revenue is earned on "exports" of services to customers outside of the Greater Vancouver region. The majority of this business is to customers located in British

Table 4.5
Percentage Distribution of Sample
Establishments Revenue by Export Markets

	Mail Questionnaire Sample (%)			Interview Questionnaire Sample (%)		
	FIRE (n=82)	Trans/Comm (n=59)	Bus.Services (n=172)	FIRE (n=25)	Trans/Comm (n=54)	Bus.Services (n=79)
Market Location						
Greater Vancouver	76	55	79	62	65	60
British Columbia	16	8	14	17	9	18
Canada	5	8	3	7	6	3
United States	1	10	1	12	9	10
Rest-of-World (ROW)	2	19	3	2	11	9

Columbia, and to a lesser extent, to customers in Canada. Only 3 percent of the sample revenue is earned on sales to customers outside of Canada. The interview sample shows a much higher degree of export revenue earned on sales outside of Canada, and sales to customers outside of British Columbia.

The transportation/communications sector is the least tied to the local Greater Vancouver market in that between 45 percent and 35 percent of the total sample revenue for this sector is earned from exports to customers located outside of the lower mainland. Between 15 percent and 16 percent of sample revenue is earned on sales to customers located in British Columbia or other Canadian provinces, and between 20 percent and 29 percent on sales to customers located outside of Canada, depending upon the sample drawn.

The business services sector shows large discrepancies in reported export activity depending upon the sample drawn. Results from the mail questionnaire show that 21 percent of the sample revenue is generated by sales outside of the Greater Vancouver region, with the vast majority of the revenue (14 percent) earned on sales within British Columbia. Only 4 percent of the sample revenue from the mail questionnaire is earned on sales outside of Canada. However, the interview sample suggests that business service establishments in the Greater Vancouver region are more nationally and internationally oriented in that 21 percent of the sample revenue for this sector was earned on sales to customers in Canada, and 19 percent from sales outside of Canada. This is a much higher level of export performance than reported in the mail questionnaire.

When all service sectors are added together, and the two samples pooled into one, it is estimated that 32 percent of the total sample revenue is earned on sales to customers located outside of the Greater Vancouver Region. This consists of 15 percent earned on sales within B.C., 5 percent on sales to customers within Canada and 12 percent on sales outside of Canada.[3] However, it must be noted that there are large discrepancies in reported export activity between the mail-out and interview samples, both for individual service sectors and when all sectors are pooled together.

The estimates of export activity are consistently higher for the interview questionnaire in comparison to the mail-out, and there are two possible explanations for this observed situation. One is simply that, in a personal interview, respondents exaggerate the importance of their export business in the same fashion that individuals often exaggerate their income or educational level during survey interviews. The second explanation is that the volume of service export activity is extremely sensitive to the establishment's structural characteristics such as size and organizational status. For example, the interview sample has a higher percentage share of headquarters and large establishments, and a lower share of locally owned establishments. If export propensities are strongly related to one or more of these factors, and the interview or mail-out sample is biased towards establishments with this characteristic, the two samples will produce different export results, and conclusions will be unduly sensitive to the process of sample selection.

The sensitivity of service export volumes to the organizational status of the sample establishments is an issue which has considerable policy relevance. This important issue has not received the attention it deserves, but some general conclusions can be drawn. In general, these data will support the hypothesis that for out-of-province exports of services, headquarter locations controlling branch offices outside the region are the most important organizational structure. Depending upon the sample drawn, and the specific service sector under investigation, single office establishments sometimes show up as earning a significant percentage of their revenue on sales outside of British Columbia, but the conclusion is quite specific to only a few of the service sectors. Finally, branch offices are shown to earn a very low proportion of their revenue on sales outside of B.C. In summary, the evidence suggests that head offices purchase an important proportion of the services consumed by their various establishments, irrespective of the geographic location of the latter, i.e., head offices act as services purchasing agent on behalf of affiliates and subsidiaries. The implications of this observation for economic development programs involving the service sector will be discussed in the next chapter.

A third issue relevant to the ultimate goal of policy analysis for the service sector concerns the age of the sample service establishments. Sixty-two percent of the establishments in the mail-out sample, and 46 percent of the establishments in the interview sample were created after 1961. The relative youth of service producing establishments is further confirmed by noting that between 25 percent and 34 percent of the sample establishments—depending upon which sample is taken—were created since 1971. The picture which emerges from these data is of a dynamic sector dominated by relatively young establishments.

Identifying the various factors which influence firms to locate in a particular region—or to choose a specific site within a region—is an important aspect for regional development for both industrial goods and service commodities, but almost no work on the topic has been done for service industries outside of Beyers' (1985, 1986) survey of Seattle-based service establishments. This issue was addressed in the interview questionnaire, but was removed from the mail-out version to lesson respondent burden. Interviewees were asked—for each of the eight reasons given in Table 4.6—to state whether the explanation suggested was very important, important, unimportant, or not relevant to the establishments location decision. Table 4.6 displays the percentage of respondents, in each of the three service sectors, who reported that the reason given was "important", i.e., very important or important, to their location decision in the Greater Vancouver Region.

Table 4.6
Reasons for Locating in the Greater Vancouver Region
by Service Sector*

	FIRE	Transportation/ Communications	Business Services
Founder lived here	62.5	34.7	74.7
Size of Vancouver market	79.2	72.0	63.4
Proximity to other markets	20.8	81.6	30.6
Access to specialized labour pools	33.3	34.7	39.4
Access to other production inputs (goods, services, transportation facilities, etc.)	29.2	71.4	33.3
Lower production costs	4.2	10.2	9.9
Personal preference for the region	75.0	34.7	68.9

* Percentage of interview sample establishments who reported the reason given to be important in their location decision.

For establishments in the FIRE sector, the most important locational variables are the size of the Vancouver market, a personal preference for the region and the simple inertia effect that the founder of the company lived in the area. Based on these data, the general picture which emerges is of a sector whose establishments are not attracted by the existence of some unique, low cost factor of production, or linkages to other market areas. Establishments in the FIRE sector more closely fit the conventional pattern of locally tied services who follow the economic activity being generated in other sectors of the economy. Establishments in the transportation/communications sector show a very different response to the various locational influences. Proximity to other markets, the size of the Vancouver market and ease of access to other production inputs are all listed as important variables in the location decision. The pattern which emerges for establishments in the transportation/ communications sectors is of a trading service sector, specifically attracted to the Greater Vancouver Region, in order to take advantage of Vancouver's geographic location relative to other major markets. Finally, the data on business service establishments show the sector to be quite similar to the FIRE sector. Establishments report that they locate in the Greater Vancouver Region because the founder lived in the area, because of a personal preference for the region and the size of the Vancouver market. This again is the typical pattern of a locally tied sector whose production input requirements can be met in any of a number of alternative market areas. The general picture which emerges from these data, especially for the FIRE and business services sectors, is of establishments who are indigenous to the local economy, in the sense that personal preferences and the size of the local economy have dominated their location decision.

The fifth result of the survey is information on the "anatomy" of a service export decision, i.e., the factors which motivated the establishment to enter into, or expand, its non-local business, the mechanism used to transact non-local service sales, and the marketing strategy used by the establishment to generate new or enhanced non-local business. Table 4.7 shows the results when respondents were asked about the factors which motivated their decision to enter into or expand non-local business. The reason receiving the highest number of positive responses was simply, "a desire to expand the business", i.e., the "pull" provided by outside markets. The second most frequently cited explanations were an unsolicited request for proposals, and the "push" effect of collapsing domestic markets, combined with the establishment's natural desire to survive. The same pattern of answers was given by all three service subsectors.

Chapter 2 discussed the importance of the mechanism, or vehicle, used to transact non-local service sales. Because a service transaction is non-tangible, the notion of trade-in-services is often thought to be without meaning unless the transaction can be accompanied with capital movement (investment), or human capital movement (transfer of people). Table 4.8 presents the interview and mail-out questionnaire results on this issue. Unfortunately, the wording of the questionnaires differed for the two samples, thus producing the "not applicable" entry in Table 4.8. The most frequently cited method by which non-local sales are generated is by direct sale in a similar fashion to the export of a physical good. The second most frequently cited mechanism is by equity investment, i.e., setting up or establishing an office to transact the business. The transfer of people and joint ventures/consortia are the next most frequently cited mechanisms. In summary, all mechanisms except franchising and subcontracting appear to be used, but the most important specific technology used to transact non-local business is simply direct export of services. All three sub-sectors show no specific deviations from this general pattern.

Table 4.7
Factors Influencing the Establishment's Entry
Into Non-Local Markets*

Reasons	Mail-Out Questionnaire (%)	Interview Questionnaire (%)
	(n = 147)	(n = 137)
Collapse of existing domestic markets	21.8	26.3
Exposure provided by Canadian sponsored projects outside of Canada	2.7	10.4
Unsolicited request for proposal	32.0	26.6
Desire to expand the business	66.7	59.9

* Percentage of sample establishments who report the reason given to be very important or important.

Table 4.8
Mechanisms Used to Transact Non-Local Business*

Reasons	Mail-Out Questionnaire (%)	Interview Questionnaire (%)
	(n = 140)	(n = 134)
Direct sales of services	55.7	70.9
Transfer of people	23.6	NA
Offices established or acquired	25.0	52.2
Franchising	5.0	NA
Joint ventures/consortia	21.4	40.2
Sub-contracting	12.9	27.3

* Percentage of sample establishments who report the reason given to be very important or important.

A third export related question concerns the marketing strategy used by the establishment to generate new or enhanced non-local business. Table 4.9 displays the results for this question. Both samples confirm that the most important way in which services are sold is by personal contacts and informal networks. Also important for both samples is direct solicitation by sales representatives. The intangible nature of the product being sold, and the tremendous possibility for significant quality differences between suppliers, implies that market information on the reputation and credibility of the supplier is extremely important. Service producers have found that the best method to supply the needed product quality information is through personal contacts and references, and use of direct solicitation by sales representatives. The other marketing strategies are important to some small group of establishments, but the wide variations in responses between samples suggests that they are unique to the characteristics of some subgroup. Particularly noticeable in the mail-out questionnaire are attendance at trade shows, advertising in printed media and direct responses to calls for tender.

Table 4.9
Marketing Strategies Used to Promote
Non-Local Service Sales*

Reasons	Mail-Out Questionnaire (%)	Interview Questionnaire (%)
	(n = 162)	(n = 137)
Advertising in printed media	17.9	62.0
Advertising in electronic media	3.7	12.4
Response for calls for tenders	25.9	51.4
Direct solicitation by sales representatives	45.7	75.0
Personal contact, references and informal networks	81.5	91.4
Attendance at trade shows, conventions, etc.	22.2	70.8

* Percentage of sample establishments who report the reason given to be very important or important.

The final issue of international and interprovincial barriers to service trade generated a wide variety of responses between samples, and over the various institutional barriers suggested to the respondents. The results for both the international and interprovincial barriers are shown in Table 4.10. Because the results for both the mail-out and interview questionnaires were not significantly different in the rankings produced, the results from the two samples have been pooled to produce a weighted average of the two instruments. The weights are the number of responses for each questionnaire. For international barriers, the most frequently cited impediment to the export of services concerns regulations inhibiting the movement of trained personnel to the foreign country, e.g., visas and work permits. The second most frequently cited barrier is the legal requirement for the exporter to obtain some sort of operating authority in the importing country, e.g., legal permission to transport goods to customers in another country, or requirements for security firms to be licensed in the importing country before accepting business from local nationals. The third most cited reason is closely related to the second, but involves licensing professionals, such as lawyers or architects, and not the firm selling the service. A fourth frequently cited impediment to exporting services from the Greater Vancouver Region is that calls for tender are limited to firms already resident in the country requesting the work. The remainder of the reasons given elicited a positive response from a small number of establishments who found them to be very important, but no general pattern applicable to the majority of establishments was obvious.

Nine possible interprovincial barriers were suggested to respondents of the mail-out and interview questionnaire. The most frequently cited interprovincial barrier was the one cited number two in the list of international barriers—the legal requirement to obtain operating authority in the province into which the establishment wishes to sell. The second and third most frequently mentioned interprovincial barriers are very close to the operating authority barrier in terms of the number of responses. Preferential purchasing practices in the buying country was not frequently cited as an international barrier, but the equivalent question in an interprovincial context, was cited by 28.5 percent of the establishments as a very important or important barrier to trade. Also, calls for tender being limited to local firms, cited number four as an international barrier, was cited number three as an interprovincial barrier. Finally, the fourth most cited interprovincial barrier was the legal requirement to hold professional certification which is issued by the host province. Thus, eliminating the barrier which has no interprovincial equivalent—the immigration and residence requirements which make it difficult to move consultants and personnel—the remaining list of frequently cited problems are remarkably similar for both inter-

Table 4.10
Institutional Barriers to the International and
Interprovincial Sale of Services*

	International Barriers	Interprovincial Barriers
	(n = 165)	(n = 191)
Calls for tender in host countries (provinces) limited to local firms	21.2	26.9
Legal requirements to obtain operating authority	35.7	29.8
Limitations to the right of establishment- national (provincial) laws restricting non-local ownership and control	11.7	11.0
Legal requirements to hold professional certification issued by the host country (province)	25.4	18.8
Preferential purchasing practices in the buying country (province)	16.0	28.5
National (provincial) regulations in the host country (province) imposing local content requirements, e.g., on labour & equipment	18.6	16.1
Legal requirements to join with local firms, e.g., joint ventures	13.0	5.0
Subsidies granted to local firms in the host country (province)	6.2	15.6
Discriminatory taxation in the host country (province) favours local firms	9.7	2.0
Registered trademark, copyright patent and industrial design protection legislation	5.6	NA
National regulations in the host country concerning immigration and residence, e.g., visas, work permits and other barriers to the movement of consultants and personnel	37.9	NA
Foreign exchange controls, e.g., barriers concerning repatriation of profits, royalties and fees	18.4	NA
National practices in the host country imposing counter trade (barter)	8.6	NA

* Weighted average of sample establishments who report the reason given to be very important or important.

national and interprovincial trade. The only difference is that preferential purchasing practices are seen to be an important interprovincial barrier to the exchange of services, but is not so frequently cited as a problem to international trade.

A closely related question asked respondents to identify not the legal or regulatory barriers which inhibit the export of services from the Vancouver region, but the more natural, economic, ones which have tended to limit their market orientation. Respondents were given nine economic barriers shown in Table 4.11. Again, responses for the mail-out and interview questionnaire have been combined because they produced very similar results. The most frequently cited reason for not getting involved in interprovincial and international export of services is that the Vancouver establishment perceived that the target provincial or foreign market is already well served by existing suppliers. In other words, local firms in other provinces or countries are able to increase domestic supply in response to any demand increase with the result that it is seen, by Vancouver-based competitors, to be difficult to obtain foreign market share. Further, it may be interpreted from this answer, that the service being provided is not sufficiently different between the two market areas that a specialist niche can be created in non-local business. The second frequently cited problem is a local production problem. Specifically, it is felt that the existing size of the Vancouver establishment, in terms of managerial and marketing capacity, cannot efficiently tolerate the increase in supply which exports would entail. Additional service production capacity can certainly be created over time, but in the short run the existing level of key inputs, such as managerial ability, would find it difficult to supervise the additional activity. Given the more uncertain nature of non-local sales, in comparison to local business, Vancouver establishments would find it difficult to make the investment in extra production capacity to serve non-local clients. The third most frequently cited reason is closely related to the results on marketing strategy. Specifically, 42.9 percent of the establishments reported that distance or communications costs inhibited personal contacts, and personal visits are an extremely important mechanism by which services are sold both domestically and to other provinces and countries. A final important point contained in Table 4.11 is that an extremely low proportion of the respondents—only 8.2 percent— ranked the level of business taxation in B.C. relative to other provinces and states to be an important impediment to their non-local sale of services.

Finally, two additional trade related issues were developed for inclusion in the interview version of the questionnaire. Establishments were asked whether or not they have recently—in the last five years—used the assistance provided by any one of five federal support programs and/or five provincial ones. The vast majority of the interviewed establishments have never used any of the support or agency programs, were unaware of their existence, or felt that the program is not applicable to the establishment. Only two programs or agencies—both federal—were cited by 20 percent or more of the interviewed establishments as having been used at least once. These two programs are the Program for Export Market Development (PEMD), and support obtained through the Canadian International Development Agency (CIDA). The final question concerned whether or not liberalized trade in services bilaterally between Canada and the United States, and multilaterally within the GATT negotiations, would increase the profitability of the interviewed service establishment. Opinions on the consequences of bilateral liberalization of trade

Table 4.11
Economic Barriers to the International and Interprovincial Export of Services*

Economic Barriers	International and Interprovincial
	(n = 265)
Insufficient size of your establishment, e.g., insufficient managerial and marketing capacity	43.1
The nature of your service (difficult to export, does not travel well)	18.0
Your establishment is not price-competitive, compared to out-of-country (province) producers	11.7
High cost of obtaining information about out-of-country (province) markets	22.4
Distance and/or communications costs inhibit personal contacts	42.9
The level of business taxation in B.C. relative to other provinces and states	8.2
Legal or organizational constraints placed on your establishment by parent company or organization	13.3
Existing market is profitable enough to meet the needs of the firms	16.8
The presence of already established competitors makes it difficult to acquire the necessary market share	46.0

* Percentages of establishments who report the reason given to be very important or important.

in services between Canada and the United States were more precise
than opinions on the multilateral version. For the bilateral question,
157 establishments answered the question, and 48 percent answered
that bilateral liberalization of trade in services would increase the
profitability of their establishment, 33 percent thought profitability
would decrease and 19 percent didn't know. With respect to
multilateral liberalization of service transactions, 156 establishments
provided an opinion, and 37 percent answered yes, 33 percent
answered no and 30 percent didn't know. Given the limited amount of
experience many establishments have with exports outside of the
United States, and the limited amount of information available on the
technical details of any agreement, it is not surprising that opinions
are evenly split, with a high uncertainty factor.

4.3   A Comparison to Seattle, Montreal, and Other Vancouver Studies

Before comparing the results from the Vancouver study to similar
studies done for the cities of Seattle and Montreal, it is insightful to
compare these findings for Vancouver to closely related work which
has also used the city as a basis of analysis.

A recent paper by Ley and Hutton (1987) examines the linkages
between advanced services located in the City of Vancouver, and the
resource extraction industries located in the province's hinterland. In
order to estimate where Vancouver based firms are buying their
service inputs—a demand side issue—interviews were conducted with
58 companies whose regional head office is in the City of Vancouver.
From these data, it was concluded that the degree of head office self-
sufficiency was remarkably high as most of 13 head office functions
identified in the questionnaire were performed both within the
corporate structure, and in the City of Vancouver. A second data set
was used by Hutton and Ley to investigate the supply side issue of
where downtown producer service firms are selling their produced
service outputs, basing their conclusions on a mail-out questionnaire
(626 replies), and an interview version (88 firms), the authors report
that customers in Vancouver absorb 71 percent of the value of output
produced by the sample firms. Non-Vancouver based B.C. resident
buyers consume 12 percent of the value of services produced by the
sample firms, while the rest of Canada and the international markets
absorb 10 percent and 7 percent respectively. These results may be
compared to the results presented in Section 4.2.3, where it was
reported that customers located in the Vancouver area absorb 68
percent of value of output produced by the sample firms. Non-
Vancouver based B.C. resident buyers are estimated to consume 15
percent of the value of services produced by all sample firms, while the
remainder of Canada and international markets absorb 5 percent and

12 percent respectively. Thus, for all three categories of market location—within B.C., within Canada and international—the two studies are quite similar, with McRae and Desbois producing higher export estimates for the B.C. and international market categories, and a lower estimate of the value of service sales to buyers located in other Canadian provinces. From these data, Hutton and Ley develop their main point of uneven development between a metropolitan core and a regional, staple product based hinterland. By noting that the provincial hinterland supplies very few services to head offices located in the metropolitan control centre, but provides markets for most of the service outputs produced by the Vancouver based firms, it is concluded that there is a growing divergence between the metropolitan and hinterland economies.

The structure and importance of service production and trade patterns for the City of Seattle has been thoroughly investigated in two reports by William Beyers et al. (1985a and 1986). The database for these studies consisted of interviews with almost 2,000 Seattle resident service establishments who estimated that exports accounted for 10 percent or more of their business revenue. Phone and personal interviews were conducted with these establishments—about 5 percent of establishments contacted refused to cooperate—to determine the volume of service exports, the factors influencing location decisions and factors influencing business success.

Several important conclusions emerge from these two research studies. First, with respect to the important issue of interregional and international trade of service commodities, the authors report that non-local sales accounted for 36 percent of the total revenue generated by the sample establishments. When non-local sales were disaggregated into three categories—outside of the Seattle area, but within Washington State; outside of Washington State, but within the United States; and outside of the U.S.—the authors report that 11 percent of total non-local revenue was earned within Washington State, 22 percent within the United States, and 3 percent from foreign countries. Thus, the level of estimated service export activity (36 percent) is remarkably close to the equivalent figure of 32 percent reported in Section 4.2.3, and 29 percent reported by Hutton and Ley. Sven Illeris (1989) has also recently computed percentages which are very similar to these. The second important point to emerge from the comparative data on market orientation concerns the relative importance of service sector exports when allocated to the three categories of non local sales. Both the Vancouver based and the Seattle based studies show approximately the same share of sales to customers located in B.C. or Washington State. However, Seattle area service firms appear to export a much higher percentage (22 percent) of the value of their output to buyers in other U.S. states in comparison to the equivalent figure for Vancouver producers. Hutton and Ley report that 10 percent of their sample revenue is earned on sales outside of B.C. but within

Canada, and this study reports a figure of 5 percent. It appears that Vancouver area service producers generate relatively little of their revenue from sales within Canada, especially in comparison to equivalent firms in Seattle. However, Vancouver area service firms rely more heavily on international sales than their Seattle based counterparts. The Seattle studies estimate international service revenue of only 3 percent, while the two Vancouver studies estimate an equivalent figure of 7 percent and 12 percent. In summary, the estimated overall importance of non local service sales is remarkably similar in both Vancouver and Seattle. However, the source of the non local revenue differs rather significantly with Vancouver firms having a more international, and less interprovincial, market orientation.

A third important hypothesis looked at by the Vancouver studies, but confirmed by the Seattle study, is that small and large service producing firms are equally active in non-local markets. In fact, the authors report absolutely no correlation between firm size and the level of non-local sales revenue. Small firms can be, and apparently are, just as active in non-local markets as large firms. This conclusion also differs slightly from the Vancouver results where it was found that larger establishments are more active in national and international markets.

A fourth conclusion confirmed from these data for Seattle based service establishments is that sales to other service producing enterprises is the major market for 36 percent of the sampled firms. Government was reported to be the major market for 17 percent of firms, and direct sales to households accounted for another 17 percent of the sample firms. Manufacturing firms were reported to be the major buyer for 12 percent of the service firms, and firms in primary industry were the most important buyer for 3 percent of the sample firms. The remaining 15 percent of the sample service producing firms reported that their major customers were located in more than one of the above categories. The importance of this observation should not be underestimated. It suggests that the growth of service exports was not primarily associated with goods production as 53 percent of the sampled firms (36 percent plus 17 percent) report that their most important buyer is either other service producers, or the public sector. The growth of service producers seems to be tied to intraservice sector demands, and not to the manufacturing sector as traditionally believed.

Regarding the question of organizational structure and interregional service trade flows, Beyers' (1986) data on service exports from Seattle illustrate a point similar to that developed by the Vancouver studies. Beyers investigates the average level of establishment revenue earned on out-of-state sales for five different types of organizational structure (regional offices; headquarters controlling external offices; single offices; headquarters lacking external offices; and branch offices). Regional offices of national firms and headquarters controlling branch offices outside the region earn a much larger proportion of their revenue outside the state of Washington in comparison to the other organizational forms. Branch offices have the lowest level of export penetration. Thus, whether the degree of interregional service flows is measured by imports or exports, the point which consistently emerges from the data is that branch offices have a high propensity to import services, and headquarter establishments— either regional or national—are large service exporters.

A sixth observation from Beyer's work confirms what was already noted for Vancouver based establishments. He notes that the most common clients identified by his sample of exporting service sector establishments are other service sector firms. On the basis of his data, Beyers (1985, p.50) concludes that:

> "This strong intra-services linkages casts doubt upon the theory that the growth of service employment has been primarily caused by the expanded demand for services as inputs to manufacturers."

Finally, Beyers' observations on the relative youth and indigenous nature of Seattle based service producing establishments are very similar to the conclusions reached for Vancouver. The youth and home-grown nature of these firms implies that they exist in a very dynamic sector of the economy.

On the whole, the picture which emerges from the Montreal studies is very similar to that for Vancouver. Business service exports for Montreal-based firms are largely destined to the rest of the province (Quebec in this case). Out of province sales to other Canadian provinces accounted for 4.9 percent of income for management consultants, 18.1 percent for advertising agencies and 10.7 percent for computer service firms in 1980 (Polèse and Léger, 1982). Foreign sales accounted, respectively, for 8.1 percent, 6.5 percent and 1.1 percent of income. Thus, Montreal's first function is that of central place for the province of Quebec, its "natural" hinterland.

This may also be confirmed by looking at the other side of the coin—service purchases by establishments outside of Montreal. Thus, for establishments surveyed in the Northern Abitibi region, 70.6 percent of business service imports originated in Montreal in the early 1980's; the respective figures were 62.3 percent for the Outaouais region; 62.2 percent for the Eastern Townships, and 51.3 percent for Thetford Mines and surroundings (Polèse, 1981). The lower figure for Thetford Mines is in large part explained by the importance of U.S. owned firms (since nationalized) in the asbestos mining sector.

The dominance of Montreal within Quebec is equally confirmed by Coffey and Polèse (1987a). The propensity to purchase services in Montreal is generally much greater for affiliated establishments in all service sectors. Purchases of financial and accounting services are especially sensitive to corporate links. However, corporate links have much less impact on trade patterns in repair, trucking and computer services. We may assume that it is those services which are related to corporate control functions, especially finance, which are most sensitive to corporate links. This in large part explains the very high concentration of financial services in cities which are also important corporate control centres.

The position of Montreal within Quebec raises some interesting questions on the role of language and provincial, or state, boundaries. The reader may find it surprising that regions such as the Abitibi, as close to Toronto as to Montreal, and l'Outaouais, just across the river from Ottawa, retain such close ties with Montreal. This pattern is equally confirmed for wholesaling purchases by retailers (Polèse, 1981). These results suggest that firms often treat Quebec as a distinct market, which warrants the existence of distinct distribution networks, including ancillary business (advertising, marketing, etc. . . .) as well as the creation of a distinct Quebec-based corporate entities.

As Coffey and Polèse (1987b) have noted, business services are very sensitive to communications costs, and in this respect language plays a role analogous to a non-tariff barrier. If the service must be delivered in French, it becomes much more costly to provide it from Toronto or Vancouver. It is equally understandable that a manager in Rouyn (in Abitibi) would prefer to deal with a French speaking provider of services, in essence lowering his communications costs, than with one in Toronto, although the latter might be "objectively" less expensive. Montreal thus, in part, enjoys a captive market for its services. However, this also means that Montreal's market will often remain regional. The rise of Toronto as Canada's primate business service centre, especially in finance, is in part linked to language and to the relative size of its home province.

Montreal has nonetheless been able to build an international export capacity in certain services, most notably engineering (Verreault and Polèse, 1988). On average, approximately half the income of Montreal-based engineering firms (Lavalin, SNC, Monenco, etc. . . .) has come from foreign projects. Because of the performance of Montreal-based engineering firms, Quebec is the only Canadian province which shows a surplus in its business service transactions with the rest of the world. The international orientation of many Montreal-based management consultants may equally be traced to the expansion of engineering firms on foreign markets. The success of engineering firms provides an interesting example, showing both the importance of public policy and of specific resource and industrial bases in the creation of regional comparative advantage in services (Polèse and Verreault, 1988). The rise of Montreal-based engineering firms is a result of important public investments in human capital (via the educational system), of Hydro Quebec's policy of out-contracting and of Quebec's geography and industrial base which permitted the development of large hydro-electrical projects.

The evidence from the Montreal studies suggests that the relationship between export capacity and ownership status is a complex one. For engineering-consulting, export earnings were almost entirely generated by locally-owned firms. The same was found to be true for computer consulting services. However, the results for management consultants and advertising agencies were much less clear-cut. Both of these sectors are in the process of rapid globalization, leading to the rise of vast international networks such as Saatchi and Saatchi, Arthur Anderson, Touche Ross, etc. Thus, it was found that foreign-affiliated establishments in these sectors often did better on international markets than purely locally controlled firms; an international consulting network such as Price Waterhouse may decide to allocate its French African contracts to its Montreal office, a concept akin to world mandates in manufacturing. Ownership links take many forms—partnerships; affiliates; subsidiaries, etc. with varying degrees of local autonomy, often making it difficult to draw a clear-cut distinction between locally and foreign-controlled establishments.

Finally, the Montreal experience shows that, as for trade in goods, cities will develop service specializations, depending on their particular locational and institutional characteristics.

4.4   Summary of the Empirical Evidence

Given the early stage of conceptual development on the issue of service sector led growth—and specifically the spatial implications of increasing service employment and output—it is perhaps not too surprising that the questionnaire based studies have provided the most policy relevant findings to date. Three conclusions stand out:

- Most service firms who "export" to customers located outside of their "urban shadow" tend to be relatively young and indigenous to the local economy. The youth and home-grown nature of these firms implies that they exist in a very dynamic sector of the economy. Unfortunately, statistically reliable estimates of the age of establishments engaged in international export of services cannot be obtained from the questionnaire based studies.

- The Seattle studies confirm the hypothesis that small firms are just as active in non-local markets as larger firms. Size is apparently not a barrier in entering non-local markets. The evidence obtained from service producing establishments in Vancouver is slightly less certain on the issue of establishment size and non-local sales. Both Vancouver based studies report weak evidence that larger than average service establishments are slightly more active in national and international markets than smaller ones. As with the establishment age variable, it is not possible to obtain reliable information on international export of services and establishment size from these questionnaire studies.

- Affiliated establishments have a much higher propensity to import services from head office locations outside the region than do independent establishments. More generally, branch offices have a high propensity to import—and low levels of export penetration—while headquarters establishments are large service exporters. In effect, head offices purchase an important proportion of the services consumed by their various establishments, regardless of the geographic location of the latter, i.e., the head office acts as a services purchasing agent on behalf of affiliates and subsidiaries.

More than any other, it is the last observation which causes us to believe that the degree to which higher order services are footloose has been significantly overestimated. The need for "face-to-face" contact remains virtually an imperative for producer services, and thus an urban centre well endowed with head office establishments is in a particularly favourable position in terms of the level of demand for local high order services. Conversely, in peripheral regions, the acquisition of locally owned firms by external interests can have a debilitating effect upon the local producer service base.

On this question of centralizing versus decentralizing tendencies, Hepworth (1987) provides some complementary information on the effects of advances in information and communications technology. He bases his conclusions on detailed case studies of nine large companies. Reflecting his interest in the information economy, attention is focussed on the effects that the introduction of computer networks in these companies have had on the spatial organization of production and distribution. The cases include large foreign subsidiaries of U.S. transnational corporations, and leading Canadian-owned firms whose operations are international in scope. Included in his list of participating firms are:

- International Business Machines (IBM) Canada
- Labatt Breweries
- Imperial Oil Canada
- Bell Northern Research
- Canadian Imperial Bank of Commerce (CIBC)
- Sears Canada
- Air Canada
- The Globe and Mail newspaper
- I.P. Sharp Associates

Less detailed case studies were conducted for three additional firms—Massey-Ferguson, Q.L. Systems, and Infoglobe.

All firms were asked to provide details on four aspects of their network operations. First, the organizational context of the firm, focussing on the firm's competitive environment and type of management decision making. Second, the technical characteristics of the computer network operated by the firm, and third, the applications, e.g., payroll or strategic decision support. Fourth, the geographic distribution of all personnel involved in developing and operating the network. It is worth quoting Hepworth (1987, p. 242) directly on the important topic of centralizing versus decentralizing tendencies inherent in the expansion of the information economy.

> "What emerges from the case study analysis is a complex "picture" of centralisation *and* decentralisation tendencies which does not provide a simple ready-made formula for new types of urban and regional economic policy. The general finding is that the economic and technical aspects of network innovations provide multi-locational firms with considerable locational flexibility in distributing various higher and lower order business functions. It is clear, nevertheless, that opportunities for major spatial restructuring will be conditioned by the ownership and control characteristics of individual firms, their product and market characteristics, and corporate responses to government policies, particularly in the important area of transborder data flow regulation."

Given the obviously complex nature of the process governing the spatial re-structuring in the Canadian information economy, Hepworth can only suggest more research, this time at the level of entire industries. At this stage, the available evidence indicates that technological advances in information and communications methods are not likely to bring about the decentralization of producer services originally forecasted. In summary, currently available data sources support the notion that the provinces which are currently the most developed and have the largest urban centres will be the ones which will most easily capture the more important dimensions of the producer service sector.

Notes

1. In Chapter 2, construction was included as part of the goods producing sector. Appendix B shows that construction and services incidental to the primary sector are both dropped from the sample due to the small number of observations.

2.   Problems with obtaining data for the group of 759 establishments classified as either banks or credit agencies other than banks resulted in them being removed from the data set. For the most part, relevant information on interregional and international transactions can only be obtained through national headquarters of these organizations.

3.   These average figures have been produced by weighting the raw percentage figures reported in Table 4.1 by the sector's share of total employment in the universe. Unweighted averages generated the same basic pattern of results, but increased the importance of sales to customers within Canada.

Chapter 5

Implications for Policy[1]

5.1 Introduction

Since the latter part of the 1970s, in both academic and government milieux, considerable optimism has been generated concerning the potential of service industries to stimulate economic development in lagging or peripheral regions. A now widely-held view suggests that service industries—along with high technology activities, in whatever manner that the latter may be defined—will ultimately aid in the solution of the long-standing economic development problems of disadvantaged regions. At the root of this optimism is the perception of these types of activities as relatively footloose; that is, free of the locational constraints that have made such regions relatively unattractive to investment in traditional forms of manufacturing. Slowly, during the early and middle 1980s, government administrative structures and policy initiatives in various countries and at various levels have begun to explicitly acknowledge the perceived capacity of service industries to influence regional economic problems (Marshall and Bachtler, 1987).

In light of the growing interest on the part of decision-makers in this sector of the economy, this chapter seeks to evaluate whether policies targeted at service activities are likely to be effective instruments of regional development, and, more specifically, to explore some of the characteristics that could potentially enhance the impact

115

of such policies. It should be noted, however, that we are dealing with only one specific policy element involving service activities: regional development. Issues of international trade, macroscale economic structural change, implications for the supply and demand of labour, and so forth will not be addressed. While most of our observations are directly related to the Canadian context, they have, in our view, a broader degree of applicability.

Our analysis begins with an examination of the role of producer services in a regional development context. This is followed by an investigation of a set of issues related to the key issue of locational flexibility, and then by an exploration of existing and potential policy interventions involving producer services and regional development.

5.2   The Role of Producer Services in Regional Development

It is the set of activities referred to as *producer services*, those intermediate demand functions that serve as inputs into the production of goods or of other services, that has the greatest potential for stimulating the economic development of lagging regions. There are four reasons why this is so. *First*, Chapter 2 showed that producer services comprise the most rapidly growing sector in the majority of developed economies. In Canada, over the period 1971-1981, employment in producer services experienced a growth rate of 141.2 percent, nearly twice that of its closest competitor, the finance, insurance and real estate (FIRE) sector. In the United States, it is estimated that 25 percent of the GNP now originates from producer services alone, the equivalent of the GNP resulting from the physical production of goods (Noyelle and Stanback, 1984). This increased demand for producer services, in turn, is a function of the changing organizational structure of goods producing activities, and of the enhanced role of product innovation and of market differentiation. That is to say, modern economies are witnessing important transformations in *what* types of goods are being produced and in *how* these goods are produced.[2]

Second, producer services can constitute an important element of the economic base of a region. As has already been discussed, according to economic base theory it is basic or export-oriented activities which serve a "propulsive" or "engine of growth" function; they create injections into the local economy which, through the multiplier mechanism and the circular flow of income, stimulate local economic growth. For many years, services had been viewed in the framework of the traditional Fisher-Clark typology of economic activity which relegated them to a "residual" category composed of "non-productive" activities. Consequently, all services had long been regarded as residentiary activities. It is now widely recognized, however, that a significant proportion of producer services, in particular, must be regarded as basic activity in that they are not only exportable, but also highly responsive to external demand. Producer services have emerged as one of the fastest growing components of both interregional and international trade. For example, Canadian based consulting and professional services, alone, accounted for $987 million worth of international exports in 1985, representing a 24-fold increase over the 1969 value (Statistics Canada, 1988). Further, at the beginning of this decade, legal services established themselves as the principal export of the New York City economy (Ginzberg and Vojta, 1981). Export-oriented business and corporate services grew at an annual rate of 10.1 percent between 1977 and 1986, attaining a total of over $50 billion in 1986, and accounting for approximately two-thirds of New York City's export earnings (Drennan, 1987).

Third, it follows from the previous point that producer services *may* be characterized by a spatial distribution that is significantly different from that of the range of residentiary, principally consumer, services. In the case of the latter, their distribution clearly follows population patterns (Marquand, 1983; Coffey and Polèse, 1988b). Due to their potential tradeability, producer services do not face the same constraint of physical proximity to their market. In theory, the less populated peripheral regions should be able to develop export-oriented producer services.

Fourth, and perhaps most importantly, through their role in investment, innovation and technological change, producer services may contribute to spatial variation in the economic development process. They may be regarded as playing a strategic role ("the locus of competitive advantage", according to Walker, 1985) within production systems of which they constitute one part of the overall division of labour. They key position that producer services occupy is essentially based upon the contribution that they can make to promoting or facilitating overall economic change and adaption. In an age of rapid technological change, certain producer services provide the source and mediators of that change (Marquand, 1983). Marshall et al. (1985) argue that producer services are an important part of the supply capacity of an economy—they influence its adjustment in response to changing economic circumstances; and they may help to adapt skills, attitudes, products and processes to changes, or to reduce the structural, organizational, managerial and informational barriers to adjustment.

In concluding this examination of the role of producer services in regional development, we make the obvious but important observation that the ability of these activities, or of any other element of the economy, to influence the level of economic development in a region is a function of the definition of development employed. If development is defined modestly in terms of incremental job creation, it may well be that public sector functions or consumer services (demand for which, in lagging regions, is perhaps largely financed by transfer payments) will be as effective an instrument as producer services. On the other hand, if development is measured in a more rigorous manner involving considerations of structural change, productivity increase, market-earned income and so forth, producer services stand virtually alone among service activities as a possible focus for policy intervention.

5.3   Trends in the Location of Producer Services: Conclusions from Theory and the Analysis of Census Data

Where the subject of producer services and regional development is concerned, the notion of *location* is of prime importance. *Where* are these high order services located?; where are they likely to be located in the future?; and what factors govern their spatial distribution? It is only those activities that are characterized by some degree of locational flexibility ("footlooseness") that are likely to enhance the economic development prospects of peripheral regions. The principal issue that needs to be examined is, therefore, that of whether high order producer services, those capable of contributing to the development of a region, are sufficiently footloose to locate in peripheral regions or, at least, outside of large metropolitan areas. This section addresses this issue by examining four of its individual elements:

- centralization, intrametropolitan deconcentration and inter-regional decentralization tendencies;
- the role of corporate ownership and control;
- the spatial separation of functions within firms; and
- the impact of telecommunications technology.

5.3.1   *Centralization, Deconcentration and Decentralization*

In both Chapter 2 of this monograph, and in the research of Coffey and Polèse (1987a; 1987c; 1988a; 1988b), a high level of spatial central-ization of producer service activities in the largest urban centres has been identified. Over the period 1971-1981, approximately 80 percent of employment growth in producer services occurred in metropolitan areas.[3] Further, more than one-half of the remaining employment growth, approximately 12 of the residual 20 percent, was located within the urban fields (a 100 km radius) of these metropolitan centres. Using location quotient analysis, Chapter 2 also showed that where producer service employment growth did occur beyond the boundaries of metropolitan areas, it was principally in the form of deconcentration, i.e. extended suburbanization, rather than a true decentralization into peripheral areas. The veritable decentralization of producer services that did take place during this period was closely related to the decentralization of traditional forms of manufacturing activity and to increased natural resource exploitation in rural areas. Further, this decentralization appears to have primarily involved standardized and routinized functions (see below).

Gillespie and Green (1987) report similar results in the British context: a centralization of producer service employment within metropolitan areas, at the national scale; and, at the intrametropolitan scale, a relative deconcentration within large urban regions. They, too, cite the varying locational trends of more and less standardized functions. Centralization trends in the location of producer services are also reported in Britain by Marshall (1982; 1985a; 1985b), Howells (1987), and Howells and Green (1986); in France by Philippe (1984) and Philippe and Monnoyer (1985); in the U.S. by Stanback et al. (1981), Noyelle and Stanback (1984), and Beyers (1988); and across a range of countries by Daniels (1985), Moss (1987), Cohen (1981), and Hall (1985).

Although an examination of the locational factors underlying these observed centralization trends in producer services is beyond the scope of this chapter, the principal determinants may be readily identified. Coffey and Polèse (1986; 1987c) have produced a model, derived both inductively and deductively, of producer service location that recognizes the contribution of three factors: a pool of highly skilled labour; complementary economic activities, largely office functions, financial institutions and complementary services; and the costs involved in "delivering" the "product" to market.[4] Taken together, these may be considered as externalities or, more precisely, economies of urbanization, which reduce the transaction costs of producer service firms. An additional factor may also be significant. Although more difficult to measure, a strong argument may be advanced concerning the role of the environment broadly defined to include social, cultural, political and physical elements in attracting the skilled labour and complementary activities referred to above. In this sense, a locality's level of public investment may be a significant factor.

5.3.2 *Corporate Ownership and Control*

As was reported in Chapter 4, the spatial pattern of corporate headquarters imposes a marked centralizing influence upon the location of producer services. More precisely, there is a high level of locational correspondence between producer service firms and the head (or divisional) offices of major corporations (Wheeler, 1988). There is strong evidence to suggest that headquarters and divisional offices purchase from sources in their direct proximity an important proportion of those services consumed by their various establishments, irrespective of the geographical location of the latter (Marshall 1982; 1985b).

As corporate control and its associated spatial division of administrative functions tend to be highly concentrated in a small number of large metropolitan areas (Noyelle and Stanback, 1984; Stanback et al., 1981; Daniels 1985; Cohen, 1981; Moss, 1987), it follows that the demand for producer services will be similarly concentrated. Therefore, an urban centre well endowed with head office establishments is in a particularly favorable position, in terms of the level of demand generated for local high order services.

The spatially proximate linkages between head office functions and the external producer service sector, and the resulting concentration of these activities within the largest metropolitan areas, are usually explained by some variant of contact theory (Tornqvist, 1970). Face-to-face contacts reflect qualitative characteristics that cannot be reproduced by long distance communication (Goddard, 1975).

Coffey and Polèse (1986) argue that the linkages between head offices and business services are becoming even stronger and more self-reinforcing than in the past. The growth of industrial concentration and corporate enterprise in itself results in a gravitation of head office activities towards the largest metropolitan areas with their diversity of producer service firms. As firms increase in size and product range, so their need for non-standardized and non-industry-specific services increases. These needs are increasingly being met by external specialized producer service firms.

The other side of the corporate control equation involves the impact upon the demand for producer services in nonmetropolitan regions. To the extent that the establishments of multiregional or multinational firms that are located in a peripheral region channel their purchases of producer services through a headquarters located in a metropolitan area—the general pattern in developed economies (Marshall 1982, 1988; Illeris, 1989) the demand for producer services in such peripheral regions will be severely constrained, particularly if the region is essentially a "branch plant" economy. In the extreme case, a branch plant of an externally controlled multinational or multi-regional firm may have no producer service linkages with the local economy.

It is therefore locally controlled or managed firms that furnish most of the demand for locally produced business services (Marshall, 1982). Where the level of local control over a regional economy is low, it follows that the potential for the development of local producer services will be modest. Regional producer service firms find it difficult to break into the multiestablishment firm market because of their small size and limited branch network.[5] The acquisition of locally owned manufacturing or resource firms by external interests can thus have a debilitating effect upon the demand for local producer service inputs. After indigenous companies are acquired, certain of their key producer service inputs are usually transferred to the new headquarters where as noted above, they are purchased from firms in the vicinity of the head office (Leigh and North, 1982).

In sum, considerations of firm creation (entrepreneurship), of head office location, and of corporate control are of vital importance for understanding the spatial distribution of producer service activities.

5.3.3 Intrafirm Functional Separation

The concept of the spatial division of labour within an economic system is now well accepted: all activities are not found in all locations. In addition, at a microeconomic scale, the division of labour *within* individual firms is increasingly taking on a spatial dimension (Massey, 1984). This is evident in the case of producer services and, indeed, of all office activities, where a clear distinction is beginning to appear between "front office" functions—higher order management tasks generally requiring face-to-face contact—and those of a "back office" nature—lower order routinized and standardized functions. The emerging consolidation and de-coupling of back office activities enables non-central locations to be utilized for these latter functions. There is general agreement in the literature, however, that the spatial separation of back office activities involves deconcentration rather than decentralization; that is to say, the "back office" of a firm is usually found on the periphery of the same metropolitan region as its "front office" (Moss, 1987; Moss and Dunau, 1986; Gillespie and Green, 1987; Nelson, 1986; Marshall, 1985b). Front office functions, on the other hand, are being increasingly centralized in a decreasing number of large metropolitan areas that are becoming functionally more specialized. At the intrametropolitan scale, these activities are becoming concentrated within the central business districts.

It is worth noting, further, that employment in the more routinized producer service functions is contracting, while employment in high order tasks is expanding (Daniels, 1987; Van Haselen et al., 1985; Moss and Dunau, 1986). Combined with the spatial separation tendencies described above, the result is that it is the largest metropolitan centres that can be expected to experience employment growth in producer services. At an intrametropolitan scale, growth can be expected to occur in the metropolitan core rather than on the periphery. These trends have the potential to create a dramatic spatial segregation of jobs according to rank, pay and gender.

There are two principal factors underlying this spatial division of labour at the intrafirm level. First, there has been an evolution in the organizational structure of firms: a shift towards more complex and advanced managerial structures which involves the relocation of high order service functions from the establishment level to the firm level. In part, this is a result of attempts to achieve scale economies and to enhance administrative control (Stanback et al., 1981). At the same time, however, this macroscale centralization is marked by a microscale separation of functions so that those activities not requiring face-to-face contact can take advantage of cost savings associated with locations not in the dense urban core of a metropolitan area.[6]

Second, the proliferation and differentiation of back office functions may be seen as a result of developments in information and communications technology (Nelson, 1986; Netherlands Economic Institute, 1986; Goddard and Gillespie, 1986). This aspect is considered in more detail in the following section.

5.3.4 *The Impact of Telecommunications Technology*

There are two major schools of thought concerning the effects of advances in telecommunications technology upon the location of high order office functions, including producer services. The first (Webber, 1973; Downs, 1985; Kellerman, 1984; Kutay, 1986, for example) reflects what might be termed the conventional wisdom: that new information and communications technology will permit the *decentralization* of office-based activities by making it possible to transact business without face-to-face contact. These technological changes will, it is argued, reduce the effects of distance and thus eliminate the differences between home and office, between city and country, and between centre and periphery.

The second school of thought adopts a viewpoint that is diametrically opposed to the first: that new information and communications technologies free office functions from the necessity of locating in proximity to the operations that they direct. This contributes to the growing *centralization* of office-based activities in a small number of metropolitan areas (subject, of course, to the separation of front and back offices at the intrametropolitan scale), while at the same time permitting the decentralization of goods producing activities into areas characterized by lower factor costs. The greater the extent of the geographic decentralization of production activities, it is argued, the greater the need for the centralization of key control activities.

While there is a paucity of empirical research on the spatial impacts of the evolution of telecommunications technology, that which does exist, on balance, lends strong support to the latter viewpoint. Hepworth (1986) demonstrates that firms in Canada are using telecommunications technology to maintain and to increase the level of spatial centralization in their organizational structures. Daniels and Thrift (1986), Goddard and Gillespie (1986), Goddard et al. (1986), Moss (1987), and the Netherlands Economic Institute (1986) similarly show that, across a range of countries, advanced information and tele-communications technology has facilitated the greater centralization, diversification and internationalization of producer services. Further, much of the empirical work cited above (e.g., Beyers, 1988; Coffey and Polèse, 1988a, 1988b; Noyelle and Stanback, 1984; Gillespie and

Green, 1987) provides indirect evidence to support this view. While not focusing explicitly on the impacts of technology, this research indicates that, during the recent period marked by significant evolution in telecommunications technology, very little decentralization has occurred. Rather, the centralization trends that have been observed in a broad set of countries have developed in parallel with, and very possibly as a direct result of, advances in telecommunications technology.

The principal factor underlying this failure of producer services and other high order office functions to behave in the manner suggested by conventional wisdom relates to the pattern of technological diffusion: there is generally a time lag in the adoption of telecommunications technologies, with the process of diffusion following the urban hierarchy. Thus, firms in metropolitan areas are able to enjoy an initial advantage in acquiring new technologies, and, due to the availability of skilled human resources, are generally better able to benefit from the options presented by the latter (Lesser and Hall, 1987; Goddard et al., 1986). The flexibility of modern technology can compensate the generally smaller firms in peripheral regions by allowing them to obtain economies of scope to replace the disadvantages of small scale, but small firms in the more highly industrialized regions also obtain this advantage. In the final analysis, the difficulty facing peripheral regions in benefitting from telecommunications advances once again reflects the traditional problems of the latter: their less diversified economic base, smaller local markets, and limited labour skills, all of which impede the rate of adoption of new technologies. Thus, the very cities that have customarily been the centres for face-to-face communication appear to be the ones that will benefit most from the spread of advanced telecommunication technologies (Moss, 1987).[7]

The evolution of telecommunications technology appears to be a two-edged sword. In theory, it does have the potential to free various types of economic activities from the locational constraints that have ruled them in the past, as well as to permit firms in peripheral regions to manage multisite organizations without establishing any part of their operations in a metropolitan area. On the other hand, however, advances in telecommunications technology enable head offices and producer service firms in large urban centres to centralize their high level management, scientific and technical functions. The problem of regional disparities in the age of new telecommunications technologies is very likely to intensify (Lesser, 1987).

In bringing this section on the trends in the location of producer services to a close, we are able to make the following observation: neither an analysis of spatial patterns across a broad set of countries, nor an exploration of the question from a more conceptual perspective indicates that there is much cause for optimism concerning the capacity for producer services to have an impact upon the level of economic development in peripheral regions. This is the underlying reality that public policy must confront. The following sections examine existing and potential policy directions is this area.

5.4   An Overview of Some Existing European Policy Initiatives

To date, the level of experience with regional policy involving services has been relatively slim. The case of the European Economic Community (EEC) countries is somewhat instructive, however, given that such policy has existed for more than 20 years. Marshall and Bachtler (1987) observe that, within the EEC, regional policy targeted on services has taken three forms. *First,* during the 1960s and early 1970s, Britain and France sought to encourage the decentralization of high order services and other office-based functions by establishing disincentives that restricted the creation of new activities of this type in large metropolitan areas. The "decentralization" that did occur involved very short distances, however: between 1963 and 1970, only 1 percent of the 70,000 jobs decentralized from London went to peripheral regions (Daniels, 1976). These policies were relaxed during the 1970s and have now mostly been abolished, as they can disadvantage both firms which need a central location, and a given metropolitan centre which is competing with other international cities.

Second, Britain, France, and the Netherlands attempted to relocate public service office functions. While this has proven to be more successful than the disincentive approach, it has primarily produced the spatial redistribution of clerical functions (Marshall and Bachtler, 1987). Further, since the general level of government expenditures has contracted recently in most countries, the possibilities for the use of this strategy have consequently diminished.

Third, during the 1970s, incentive policies were introduced. These involved, on the one hand, the creation of service-specific incentives (e.g., in Britain, France, and Ireland, employee transfer grants, rent relief, capital grants, training and job creation grants) and, on the other hand, the extension of existing regional incentives to include services. Both approaches tended to be restricted to service firms with a choice of location ("mobile offices"), or with a certain proportion of exports outside the destination region. Alternatively, in a variation upon the "picking winners" theme, attempts were made to identify specific sectors of major national significance, in terms of export orientation or job creation, and to provide support to them. Among the difficulties encountered with the incentive approach were low funding priorities, low levels of assistance, and a lack of publicity (Marshall and Bachtler, 1987).

An issue related to the creation of a service-specific regional policy involves the implementation of a supply-side service approach to regional development. Here, the reasoning is that government policies to expand the supply of producer services in specific peripheral regions will attract other types of industries and, hence, increase the level of economic development. Towards the beginning of the 1980s both academics (e.g., Marshall, 1982; Goddard, 1980) and governmental organizations (Northern Region Strategy Team, 1977) advocated such an approach, arguing that is could be more easily pursued by government than the traditional forms of regional policy, since the financial encouragement involved need be less substantial. During the course of the decade, this strategy was implemented to some degree in several countries, but at this time it is not clear to what extent the policy has been successful. It is perhaps significant, however, that the more recent literature has not dealt with this approach.

An important impetus towards the development of service-specific policies has been provided by the changing economic context created by the recession of the early 1980s. Most developed countries are now witnessing a greater emphasis on national innovation and science policies, and the restriction of public expenditure. While regional development policy *per se* has come under strong pressure, the level of interest in service activities has increased due to the perceived ability of the latter to provide low cost job creation, particularly at a time when manufacturing's contribution to employment growth is limited. This has recently resulted in a more favorable treatment for services in the context of existing regional policy (e.g., Germany, Ireland, Britain, Italy) and in the introduction of new service incentive schemes (e.g., France).

After the more than 20 years of experience with some form of regional policy targeted on service activities, European initiatives in this area cannot be qualified as conspicuously effective in generating development or, even more narrowly, in creating employment in lagging regions (Marshall and Bachtler, 1987). The emphasis upon services in regional policy remains tentative and, in some instances, may be regarded as cosmetic. Marshall (1985a) posits that there are several likely explanations for this lack of success: the continued focusing of assistance upon manufacturing industry; an incomplete understanding of the economics of the service sector; the fact that much service employment is tied to levels of local consumer expenditure and that, thus far, regional policies intent on creating additional employment have not been able to satisfactorily distinguish these locally-tied services from tradeable ones; and the spatial concentration of corporate control and the associated division of administrative functions between office sites and subordinate organizational units. A further problem is that the overwhelming majority of service policies are conceived in isolation, in the sense of not considering the interdependence between high order services and other forms of economic activity (Marshall, 1988; Illeris, 1989).

The prospects for service-oriented regional initiatives must also be viewed in light of the existing policy context in most developed countries, where regional and national policies are often in direct opposition, with the latter generally providing assistance to firms in more prosperous areas. Marshall (1985a) notes that where national policies towards services exist, they tend to contradict the goals of regional policy: assistance is channelled to the more developed regions. On the other hand, as noted, although services are now eligible for mainstream regional development assistance in most countries, expenditure on regional policy is declining.

In sum, based upon the European experience, the prognosis is not highly positive. The impact of a service-oriented regional policy on peripheral areas could be quite modest. It is unlikely that government policies of any type will be able to combat the observed centralizing tendencies of high order producer services (Marshall, 1985b). While there is a case for including producer services in a regional development policy on the grounds of their contribution to employment creation, such policy must confront the fact that employment growth in such activities has not benefitted central and peripheral areas equally. This does not suggest that an emphasis upon services in regional policy is entirely impractical. For it to be effective, however, it will need to have access to more resources, and to be more sophisticated than past attempts. In the following section, we present some ideas concerning the specific directions that such policies might take.

5.5   Producer Services: Appropriate Policy Intervention

5.5.1 Framework Policies

It follows from the empirical and conceptual evidence reviewed thus far that, in most instances, services cannot be regarded as the answer to the economic development problems of lagging regions, many of which are small and geographically peripheral. Although there are specific exceptions, and although there are *relative* trends towards decentralization observable, high order services—those with a high propensity for export and, therefore, for the stimulation of economic growth—generally continue to be highly concentrated in major urban centres. Nevertheless, it is useful to explore some of the essential elements that a service-oriented regional strategy might include. In presenting these ideas, we draw heavily upon our own research on the Canadian space-economy and, as well, upon the international literature.

Perhaps the first point that needs to be made concerns the complementarity between goods production and producer services. A number of authors (Gershuny, 1978; Gershuny and Miles, 1983; Noyelle and Stanback, 1984; Stanback et al., 1981; Bailly and Maillat, 1988) have conclusively demonstrated the close interdependence of physical production and high order services; the latter may correctly be regarded as an integral element of any modern production process. It therefore follows that a regional policy aimed either at "productive" activities (i.e., primary and secondary activities) or at producer services, in isolation, will be destined to a suboptimal degree of effectiveness. Regional policy towards both will need to be integrated.

Stated in slightly different terms, regional policy must concern itself with both supply side and demand side aspects of producer services in lagging regions. Supply side incentives will only be effective if there is a demand for the service that is produced. In most instances, this will involve local demand, since producer service firms in peripheral regions cannot be realistically expected to export a large proportion of their output in the short term. Thus an important constraint upon the development of producer services in such areas is the poor performance of indigenous non-service industries, and the internalization of demand within large firms. This problem will not be easily resolved by the supply side policy; a more proactive approach is necessary on the demand side.

More tangibly, a supply side approach needs to include such measures as human resource policies designed to create a pool of skilled labour in a given region and, at a different scale of organization, incentives aimed at the creation of producer service firms themselves. In theory, a substantial supply of skilled labour will assist a region in attracting or in generating high order producer service, and other knowledge intensive, firms. In addition to training and education initiatives, human resource policies may also include measures designed to improve the social-cultural-political environment of a given city, thus making it more attractive to the highly skilled labour force. Similarly, the presence of a range of producer service firms may enable a region to attract or to create complementary, i.e., non-service forms of economic activity.

The demand side approach consists of generating sufficient demand to stimulate the initial creation and subsequent growth of high order service firms. The growth of engineering services in Quebec is a particularly good example of this strategy (see below). Another element involves regional import substitution in producer services— the encouragement of externally owned firms operating in a region to increase their purchase of locally produced services. In this manner one can attempt to avoid the classic "branch plant economy syndrome" in which multinational or multiregional firms operating in a region have virtually no backward linkages with the local economy. One must be extremely careful that import substitution policies do not degenerate into simple protectionist programs, and thus compromise the basic principles of allocative efficiency, but a selective and temporary program of using import information to help identify market opportunities for local suppliers may be possible. Similarly, a regional strategy towards the creation of local business might require that the latter make significant use of local services.

Either a supply side or a demand side approach, in isolation, is a fragile one. If policy intervention is to be attempted, both avenues need to be pursued simultaneously. It is, for example, well and good to pursue human resource policies, but if parallel efforts are not made to stimulate the demand for this resource the result will likely be the out-migration of the newly created skills.

The analysis presented in this monograph suggests that the historical neglect of service industries from public sector support has probably been justified *insofar as regional balance is concerned.* Although there are specific exceptions, and although there are trends towards relative decentralization observable, high order services, i.e., those with a high propensity for export and thus for the stimulation of economic growth, generally continue to be highly concentrated in major urban centres. The possibilities for the development of high order services in nonmetropolitan regions thus appear to be limited to the following:

- producer services that respond to the demands of local economic activities, i.e., local manufacturing or primary sector firms;

- producer services that respond to local public sector demand;

- standardized and routinized "back office" services, e.g., data processing or mail order functions; and

- specialized and tradeable services which are derived from long term, local expertise in the primary or manufacturing sectors.

In the case of the first and second options, services are fulfilling a principally residentiary function. They may, however, assist the economic growth of the local economy to the extent that they create jobs and that they may be substituted for higher cost/lower quality imports from outside of the region. Option 3 may be important in the provision of employment opportunities in a local area, but is unlikely to stimulate economic growth. Option 4 represents the only real potential for export development.

The current expertise, and predominant position, of Quebec-based engineering consulting firms is a useful concrete example of this phenomenon and, as such, warrants a brief summary. In the 1960s and 1970s, partially in order to resolve and/or to avoid union problems, Hydro-Québec, a provincial Crown corporation, began to use the services of independent firms to provide the engineering and management for their vast hydroelectric projects. This contracting-out strategy is clearly one of the major factors—along with an enhanced educational system that was able to assure a supply of highly skilled human resources—in the success story of the Quebec engineering consulting sector. Due to this decision, local firms, at first in cooperation with external partners such as the American giant Bechtel, were able to simultaneously establish a viable level of activity, to develop a base of expertise, and to acquire foreign technology. Over time, this combination has propelled several Quebec firms, which now work without foreign assistance, e.g., Lavalin, SNC, to the status of major actors in the global context. The evolution of the Quebec engineering sector may be contrasted with that of Ontario, whose Crown corporation, Ontario Hydro, chose to maintain a large internal engineering department (Verreault and Polèse, 1988).

Further information on this topic is provided for the Canadian mining and metallurgy industry by Richardson (1987). Data compiled from industry sources by Richardson indicate that there are over 250 firms in Canada active in the sale of mining expertise. The principal vehicles by which Canadian mineral expertise is sold abroad is via consulting firms which exist specifically for this purpose. However, large Canadian mining companies such as Inco and Noranda have also established mechanisms to market their proprietary technologies abroad.

The activities of the 250 firms directly engaged in the sale of expertise cover a broad range of mining and metallurgical operations with heavy emphasis on mineral exploration, mine design, mine development, underground mining and open-pit mining. For the most part, however, the Canadian firms have restricted their involvement to the generation of reports and feasibility studies, and to mine construction management. They tend not to be involved in the "downstream" activities of mine construction or mine operation management. Entry into the total service segment of the market, i.e., the entire package of services including engineering, procurement, construction and start-up operations, has historically been denied to Canadian firms due to the lack of Canadian based world-scale consulting engineering corporations. However, the growth of companies such as Lavalin, Wright Engineering and SNC have eliminated this deficiency, and recently allowed Canadian mining and metallurgy companies to compete against large U.S. and Japanese firms for full service contracts. Examples include the development of the Tintaya open pit copper mine in Peru by a consortium headed by the SNC group, and the construction of a sulphuric acid complex in Mexico by a group headed by Lavalin-Fenco Inc.

Finally, the need for locationally-specific policies must be stressed. Our research on the Canadian space-economy suggests that small and medium-sized cities (in the 25,000 - 100,000 population range) that are not in the zone of influence of a large metropolitan centre have some potential for the development of producer service activities to serve local demand. Centres within the "shadows" of major urban areas, and places below this size threshold do not appear to have such potential, although the possibility that such areas will be able to develop highly specialized service "niches" should not be overlooked. Thus, *if* a regional policy based upon high order service activities is to be attempted, it needs to be tailored according to the characteristics of individual areas; a blanket approach will likely prove to be highly counter-productive.

5.5.2 *An Exploration of More Specific Policy Responses*

When attention is turned from the general identification of "framework" type policies for producer services to the more detailed issue of policy goals, it is tempting to begin by using the established program elements historically used to support the manufacturing sector. There are six program elements which have been part of the Industrial and Regional Development Program (IRDP) applied to manufacturing. These are:

- business development climate
- innovation
- establishment
- modernization/expansion
- marketing
- restructuring

In addition to these program elements, which form the backbone of the IRDP, there are a variety of programs run by other federal government departments, and by all of the provincial governments. However, even though the exact choice of development instrument varies by province and department—e.g., the Federal Business Development Bank (FBDB) uses a host of financial aid and management service instruments—the goals of all the development programs are adequately summarized by the six IRDP program elements.

From the analysis presented to date, it follows that service industries which potentially qualify for program support—tradeable specialized services derived from long-term expertise in the primary or manufacturing sectors—can benefit most from two of the program elements identified in the IRDP grouping. The *first* is establishment assistance. The evidence produced from questionnaire based studies points very strongly to the fact that many of the producer service firms which are strategically important for regional and urban development are relatively young. It is the start-up of new firms, and to a lesser extent the expansion of recently started businesses, that provides much of the employment growth in this sector. A similar point on the importance of service sector start-ups is presented by the Ontario Study of the Service Sector (1986, p.36),

"While the service sector accounts for well in excess of 80 per cent of all new jobs created in Ontario, various studies appear to confirm that births of new firms—rather than expansions of established ones—in turn account for by far the largest share of those new service sector jobs. The Ministry of Industry, Trade and Technology estimates, for instance, that births of new businesses accounted for 71 per cent of all new service sector jobs created between 1976 and 1985."

Thus, the first relevant goal for public sector support programs is to help increase the establishment, and reduce the failure rate, of targeted producer service businesses.

In order to achieve this first goal, two development instruments should be considered. The first is financial assistance. Many of the firms in the producer services sector point out that as service firms they do not have access to the usual channels of capital lending. This problem arises because most collaterilized loan packages offered by private institutions are geared to relatively large manufacturing concerns with major capital investments. Service firms often find adequate financing difficult to obtain because their primary collateral is not physical assets, but their experience, education, managerial and professional abilities. Interview results suggest that the problem is most severe in service industries such as insurance, transportation, health industries and some engineering and research fields which require relatively large start-up investments, and for firms in the early phases of their development. Firms which require cash flow assistance for expansion purposes, and firms in law, accounting, architecture, engineering, consulting etc., which have relatively low capital requirements when starting out, are able to rely more on private loan institutions, or family funds. It is clear that the lack of a well established loan network for many service sector firms has not completely strangled the development of these firms. However, many are prematurely lost—a point noted by the Ontario Study of the Service Sector (1986, p.39)—and newer service firms may experience a greater need for capital assistance than older firms. This follows from the ever increasing start-up capital requirements as technology becomes a more integral component in service production, e.g., the use of computer aided design systems in engineering and architecture, and the need to match existing and potential competitors on a global basis.

The second development instrument relevant to the goal of business establishment is information availability. Relevant, up-to-date information on trends in the regional economy, demographic patterns, new interregional or international export opportunities and general management advice are in great demand by service sector firms, especially the smaller ones who have neither the time nor the resources to obtain this information at commercial rates. Also important to service sector firms is information on the availability, terms and conditions under which publicly provided support programs are available. Thus, information relevant to both sound business decisions and operations, and relevant to available support programs should be available on a decentralized basis through a single agency of government.

The *second* major program element which is critically important to tradeable, specialized service firms which have a link to local primary or manufacturing expertise, is marketing assistance. Marketing for interregional and international sales of service outputs differs from equivalent marketing efforts for goods in two significant ways.

The first concerns the mechanism by which the exchange takes place. For physical goods, interregional or international exchange takes place by the direct movement of the good, e.g., dimension lumber is shipped from Vancouver to San Francisco. However, for many services the method or vehicle by which the exchange takes place is much more varied. In addition to the direct export of service outputs, e.g., data transmitted by telecommunications from one country to the other, Chapter 4 made clear that there are five additional ways by which services may by exchanged interregionally or internationally.

- Some services which are not storable and transportable— examples include banking, insurance, motor and air transport—require a direct investment to create and maintain an establishment abroad.

- In sectors such as engineering, management consulting, advertising, and repair work, service outputs may be traded across borders only by the temporary movement of skilled personnel.

- For other service sectors, the vehicle by which they enter into interregional or international trade is in a form embodied in some physical output. For example, computer operating software—a service output—is increasingly dominating hardware in terms of total system value, but can only be sold as a package embodied in the physical export. Other examples include books and films whereby the service activity of acting or writing can only be exported through the physical form of books and films.

- A fourth mechanism for exporting services is closely related to the direct investment vehicle, but involves non-equity forms of investment such as franchising, leasing, licensing agreements, and subcontracting. The purpose is to use someone else's brand name, advertising or distribution network. For the privilege of using this service, a payment is made to the owner of the service and is recorded as an "export" if income is received from non-residents.

- Finally, an important category of interregional and international service trade is classified as "establishment trade", i.e., service transactions performed by manufacturing and primary resource firms as intraestablishment sales of head office services such as advertising, accounting, data processing, software and legal services. These service output sales are not arm's length transactions, but instead are intra-establishment exchanges done within the umbrella of a multi-branch corporation.

With such a rich and varied set of exchange mechanisms the associated problems of marketing—product strategy, distribution, price and promotion strategies—become much more complex in comparison to the problems faced by a goods exporter who has only one interregional or international exchange mechanism.

Marketing for service outputs also differs from goods due to the intangible nature of the product. Because of the intangibility of service outputs, it is often difficult for the buyer to certify product quality. Fortunately, there are several formal and informal market mechanisms to deal with the domestic and international problems of quality assurance. Fee schedules can be designed to make the level of fees paid contingent upon the successful and complete delivery of the service. This market mechanism works so long as all attributes of the service are visible and can be monitored. Also, warranties and performance bonds can be used in the same contingent fashion to provide assurance to the buyer that potential problems with poor quality can be incorporated prior to making the decision to purchase. Finally, certification and monitoring of the service provider—either by a public body or by the service providing industry itself—also provides a mechanism to deal with potential quality problems.

However, the most common way in which quality assurance is built into national and international service sales is through the establishment and protection of a good reputation by the seller. The importance of reputation as a mechanism for quality assurance, and hence successful marketing, is confirmed in Chapter 4 for Vancouver-based service establishments, and by Beyers (1985a) in his work in Seattle. Reputation and references are the most dominate market strategy, easily outdistancing direct solicitation by sales representatives, the second most frequently mentioned marketing technique. The relevant public policy question with respect to reputation is whether the market by itself, and operating within the structural characteristics of the Canadian marketplace, is able to generate and distribute enough of it. It may legitimately be argued that many regional Canadian service producers have not been able to generate national and international reputations sufficient to help produce service quality assurance. See McRae in McRae and Desbois (1988) for a more technical discussion of this issue.

Many reputation-enhancing development instruments are potentially available to the public sector. Demonstration projects, government procurement, performance bonding, help with "errors and omission" insurance, help in creating export consortia, and taking the role of prime contractor in government to government deals have at various times, and for various service subsectors, been suggested as ways in which the public sector can help remove impediments to the growth of Canadian service firms. The common theme of all is that they aim to enhance the national and international credibility of Canadian firms.

Finally, there is a *third* important program element which is not part of the IRDP package because it is unique to the service sector. The Ontario Study of the Service Sector (1986, p.18) points out that,

> "Education is as vitally fundamental an element of public infrastructure in the new knowledge-based economy as roads, railways, ports and power sources were in the previous predominantly manufacturing-oriented one."

Education is the single most important input in almost all producer service industries, and hence, should become a program element in any future government support programs targeted on the service sector.

The curriculum and fiscal issues relevant to education is an immensely complex area, involving inputs from nearly all dimensions of Canadian society, not just the service sector. However, the specific needs of services—mainly the producer services subsector—are typical of all industries who are, or will be, part of the information revolution.

Three "needs" deserve attention in any policy initiatives directed at the educational needs of the service sector:

- The need for the primary and secondary school system to ensure that the curriculum teaches flexibility, the ability to think, and make independent decisions. The non-standardized nature of many important producer services requires individuals who are capable of drawing upon their basic education in order to deal with constantly changing situations.
- The need of the university and college system to address the requirements of local service industries in terms of teaching specific skills. Examples include the various dimensions of the design sector, the hospitality, insurance and real estate sub-sectors.
- The need for increased levels of financial support for basic research at universities and other independent research organizations. The road from basic research to commercialization is long and complicated, involving the cooperation of many organizations and individuals. However, the process begins with universities and other research institutes which

generate the technology base, and become the magnets around which complementary industries will cluster.

5.6 Conclusion

The evidence that we have presented in this chapter suggests that the conventional wisdom concerning the capability of "footloose" service activities to enhance the economic development prospects of peripheral regions is unjustifiably optimistic. The potential for high order producer services to locate outside of major metropolitan centres is highly limited. The main locational shifts of producer services that most developed economies are witnessing are occurring primarily at the intrametropolitan level (Marshall, 1988; Nelson, 1986; Moss and Dunau, 1986). In terms of specific policy interventions to stimulate service activities in lagging regions, considerable caution must be exercised. It is not at all clear that such interventions will have a high probability of success. Even more than in the case of manufacturing, the forces of spatial concentration are very strong.

Attempts to create an effective service policy for peripheral regions need to be grounded in a better understanding of the economics of high order services and, particularly, of the factors governing the location of these activities. Further, such considerations cannot be divorced from the broader issues concerning the future of regional policy, the greater integration of national science and technology policies with regional policy, and new forms of international competition. Perhaps even more fundamentally, we are led once again to the classic existential question of the regional development practitioner—is it really worthwhile to expend so much effort in attempting to resist the "natural" market trends?

Notes

1. Certain revised portions of this chapter formed the basis for a paper presented by William Coffey and Mario Polèse at the North American Meetings of the Regional Science Association in November 1988, entitled "Producer Services and Regional Development: A Policy Oriented Perspective". This paper will be published in a forthcoming issue of the *Papers* of the Regional Science Association.

2. It must also be recognized that, due to the strategies of individual firms in internalizing or externalizing certain management-related functions—the overall trends in the organizational structure of firms being to promote increasing externalization—the extent of the growth of free-standing producer service activities may represent an over-estimation. For example, when a manufacturing firm decides to replace internalized accounting or legal functions with those purchased from external producer service firms, the extent of the producer service *function* in the economy has not grown, although the statistics show a net shift from manufacturing towards producer service employment. This has led some authors (McRae, 1985) to argue that some of the observed growth of producer services and, more generally, of the entire range of service activities is largely a statistical

artifact. On the other hand, however, it can be argued that the producer service *function*, as opposed to *sector*, is underrepresented due to the internalization of these activities in many goods producing firms. Recent evidence (Tschetter, 1987), however, has indicated that producer service growth is far from being a statistical artifact.

3.　The highest *rates* of growth were found in rural regions and smaller urban places, but these high growth rates translated into relatively small absolute change. Metropolitan areas, on the other hand, experienced more modest growth rates that manifested themselves in large absolute increases. Due to the difference between the relative and absolute performance of both metropolitan and nonmetropolitan areas, the situation may be characterized as one of relative demetropolitanization, but absolute centralization.

4.　The relative importance of the first two elements to an individual establishment is related to its preference for the internalization or the externalization of knowledge-related inputs. This choice, in turn, is a function of considerations related to levels of confidentiality, standardization, and the uncertainty of the economic environment under which the establishment operates.

5.　It may further be noted that local branch offices of national producer service firms add to regional employment, but those with limited autonomy carry out predominantly marketing and brokerage tasks, and their local multiplier effect is thus limited.

6.　While our discussion has focused primarily on producer service firms themselves, it is clear that analogous developments in the management functions across the whole range of economic activities have contributed to trends in the producer service sector. The external purchase of all but industry-specific services is now recognized as a preferred strategy to reduce overall production costs.

7.　Advances in telecommunications technology have increased, rather than diminished, the demand for face-to-face contact in large metropolitan centres (Netzer, 1977), and have extended the geographic reach of individuals and firms in these cities (Moss, 1987).

References

Bailly, A.S. and D. Maillat, 1988. *Le secteur tertiaire en question*, 2nd ed. Geneva: Editions Régionales Européennes.

Baumol, W.J., 1967. "Macroeconomics of Unbalanced Growth: The Anatomy of Urban Crisis", *American Economic Review*, 57, pp.415-26.

Baumol, W.J., S.A. Blackman, and E.N. Wolff, 1985a. "Unbalanced Growth Revisited: Asymptotic Stagnancy and New Evidence", *American Economic Review*, 75, pp.806-17.

Baumol, W.J., 1985b. "Productivity Policy and the Service Sector", in Robert Inman (ed.) *Managing the Service Economy: Prospects and Problems*, New York: Cambridge University Press, pp.301-17.

Beyers, W.B., M.J. Alvine and E.G. Johnson, 1985a. *The Service Economy: Export of Services in the Central Puget Sound Region.* Seattle, Wash.: Central Puget Sound Economic Development District.

Beyers, W.G. and M.J. Alvine, 1985b. "Export Services in Postindustrial Society", *Papers of the Regional Science Association*, 57, pp.33-45.

Beyers, W.B., J.M. Tofflemire, H.A. Stranahan and E.G. Johnson, 1986. *The Service Economy: Understanding Growth of Producer Services in the Central Puget Sound Region.* Seattle, Wash.: Central Puget Sound Economic Development District.

Beyers, W.B., 1988. "Trends in the Producer Services in the U.S.: The Last Decade". Paper presented at the annual meeting of the Association of American Geographers, Phoenix, AZ, April.

Burgess, D.F., 1987. "Trade in Services and the Foreign Direct Investment Process: Some Implications from the Specific Factors Model." Discussion Paper. Victoria, B.C.: Institute for Research on Public Policy.

Clark, C., 1940. *The Conditions of Economic Progress*, London, Macmillan.

Coffey, W.J. and M. Polèse, 1986. "The Interurban Location of Office Activities: A Framework for Analysis", in D.J. Savoie (ed.), *The Canadian Economy: A Regional Perspective.* Toronto: Methuen, pp.85-103.

_____, 1987a. "The Distribution of High Technology Manufacturing and Services in the Canadian Urban System, 1971-1981", *Revue d'économie régionale et urbaine*, no. 5, pp.279-99.

_____, 1987b. "Intra-firm Trade in Business Services: Implications for the Location of Office-Based Activities", *Papers of the Regional Science Association*, 62, pp.71-80.

_____, 1987c. "Trade and Location of Producer Services: A Canadian Perspective", *Environment and Planning A*, 19, 5, pp.597-611.

Coffey, W.J. and M. Polèse, 1988a. "Locational Shifts in Canadian Employment, 1971-1981: Decentralization versus Decongestion", *The Canadian Geographer*, 32, pp.248-56.

_____, 1988b. *Service Activities and Regional Development in Canada: Patterns, Theory, and Policy.* Unpublished report submitted to the Institute for Research on Public Policy.

Cohen, R., 1981. "The New International Division of Labour, Multinational Corporations and Urban Hierarchy", in M. Dear and A. Scott (eds.), *Urbanization and Urban Planning in Capitalist Society.* New York: Methuen.

Curtis, D. and K. Murthy, 1988. "Modeling the Dynamics of Structural Change in the Aggregate Economy". Unpublished manuscript presented to the International Atlantic Economic Conference, London, England.

Daniels, P.W., 1976. "Office Employment in New Towns", *Town Planning Review*, 47, pp.210-24.

_____, 1985. *Service Industries: A Geographical Appraisal.* London: Methuen.

_____, 1987. "The Geography of Services", *Progress in Human Geography*, 11, 3, pp.433-47.

Daniels, P.W. and N.J. Thrift, 1986. *Producer Services in an International Context.* University of Liverpool Working Paper on Producer Services, no. 1.

Dobell, A.R., J.J. McRae and M. Desbois, 1984. "The Service Sector in the Canadian Economy: Government Policies for Future Development", Discussion Paper, Victoria, B.C.: Institute for Research on Public Policy.

Dobell, A.R. and J.J. McRae, 1985. "The Contribution of Service Attributes to Trade Performance", Discussion Paper, Victoria, B.C.: Institute for Research on Public Policy.

Downs, A., 1985. "Living With Advanced Telecommunications", *Society*, 23, 1, pp.26-34.

Drennan, M., 1987. "New York in the World Economy", *Survey of Regional Literature*, no. 4, pp.7-12.

Economic Council of Canada, 1978. *A Time for Reason*, 15th Annual Review, Ottawa: Supply and Services Canada.

_____, 1984. *Western Transition*, Ottawa: Supply and Services Canada.

Fisher, A.G.B., 1935. *The Clash of Progress and Society.* London: Macmillan.

_____, 1939. "Production: Primary, Secondary and Tertiary", *The Economic Record*, 15, pp.24-38.

Fuchs, V.R., 1968. *The Service Economy.* New York: National Bureau of Economic Research.

Gershuny, J.I., 1978. *After Industrial Society: The Emerging Self Service Economy.* London: Macmillan.

Gershuny, J.I. and I.D. Miles, 1983. *The New Service Economy.* London: Frances Pinter.

Gillespie, A.E. and A.E. Green, 1987. "The Changing Geography of Producer Services Employment in Britain", *Regional Studies*, 21, 5, pp.397-411.

Ginzberg, E. and G.J. Vojta, 1981. "The Service Sector of the U.S. Economy", *Scientific American*, 244, 3 (March), pp.48-55.

Goddard, J.B., 1975. *Office Location in Urban and Regional Development*. Oxford: Oxford University Press.

_____, 1980. "Industrial Innovation and Regional Economic Development in Britain". DP-32, Centre for Urban and Regional Development Studies, University of Newcastle-upon-Tyne.

Goddard, J.B. and A.E. Gillespie, 1986. *Advanced Telecommunications and Regional Development*. Newcastle-upon-Tyne: Centre for Urban and Regional Development Studies.

Goddard, J.B., A. Gillespie and F. Robinson and A. Thwaites, 1986. "The Impact of New Information Technology on Urban and Regional Structure in Europe", in A. Thwaites and R. Oakey (ed.), *The Regional Impact of Technological Change*. London: Francis Pinter, pp.215-41.

Gottmann, J., 1977. "Megalopolis and Antipolis: The Telephone and the Structure of the City". In I. de Sola Pool (ed.), *The Social Impact of the Telephone*. Cambridge, MA.: MIT Press, pp.303-17.

Hall, P., 1985. "The World and Europe", in J. Brotchie, P. Newton, P. Hall and P. Nijkamp (eds.), *The Future of Urban Form*. Sydney: Croom Helm.

Hepworth, M., 1986. "The Geography of Technological Change in the Information Economy", *Regional Studies*, 20, 5, pp.407-24.

Hepworth, M., 1987. *The Geography of the Information Economy: A Study of Technical and Economic Change in Canada*. Unpublished Ph.D dissertation submitted to the University of Toronto.

Howells, J., 1987. "Developments in the Location, Technology and Industrial Organization of Computer Services: Some Trends and Research Issues", *Regional Studies*, 21, 6, pp.493-503.

Howells, J. and A.E. Green, 1986. "Location, Technology and Industrial Organization in U.K. Services", *Progress in Planning*, 26, pp.85-183.

Illeris, S., 1989. *Services and Regions in Europe*. Aldershot: Gower.

Inman, R.P., 1985. "Introduction and Overview", in R. Inman (ed.), *Managing the Service Economy: Prospects and Problems*, New York: Cambridge University Press, pp.1-24.

Jones, R.W. and F. Ruane, 1987. "Options for International Trade in Services: A Specific Factors Framework." Discussion Paper. Victoria, B.C.: Institute for Research on Public Policy.

Kellerman, A., 1984. "Telecommunications and the Geography of Metropolitan Areas", *Progress in Human Geography*, 8, 2, 222-46.

Kendrick, J.W., 1985. "Measurement of Output and Productivity in the Service Sector", in R. Inman (ed.), *Managing the Service Economy: Prospects and Problems*, New York: Cambridge University Press, pp.111-23.

Kutay, A., 1986. "Effects of Telecommunications Technology on Office Location", *Urban Geography*, 7, 3, pp.243-57.

Kuznets, E., 1966. *Modern Economic Growth: Rates, Structure, Spread*. New Haven: Yale University Press.

_____, 1971. *Economic Growth of Nations*. Cambridge: Harvard University Press.

Leigh, R. and D. North, 1978. "The Spatial Consequences of Take-overs in Some British Industries and Their Implications for Regional Development", in F.E.I. Hamilton (ed.), *Contemporary Industrialization: Spatial Analysis and Regional Development*. London: Longman, pp.158-81.

Lesser, B., 1987. "Technological Change and Regional Development", in W.J. Coffey and M. Polèse (eds.), *Still Living Together: Recent Trends and Future Directions in Canadian Regional Development*. Montreal: Institute for Research on Public Policy.

Lesser, B. and P. Hall, 1987. *Telecommunications Services and Regional Development*. Halifax: The Institute for Research on Public Policy.

Ley, D. and T. Hutton, 1987. "Vancouver's Corporate Complex and Producer Services Sector: Linkages and Divergence within a Provincial Staple Economy", *Regional Studies*, 21, pp.413-24.

Magun, S., 1982. "The Rise of Service Employment in the Canadian Economy", *Relations Industrielles*, 37, pp.528-56.

Mansell, R.L., 1985. "The Service Sector and Western Economic Growth", *Canadian Public Policy*, Supplement, II, pp.354-60.

Markuson, J.R., 1987. "Trade in Producer Services: Issues Involving Returns to Scale, and the International Division of Labour." Discussion Paper. Victoria, B.C.: Institute for Research on Public Policy.

Marquand, J., 1983. "The Changing Distribution of Service Employment", in J.B. Goddard and A.G. Champion (eds.), *Urban and Regional Transformation of Britain*. London: Methuen, pp.99-134.

Marshall, J.N., 1982. "Linkages Between Manufacturing Industry and Business Services", *Environment and Planning A*, 14, pp.1523-40.

_____, 1985a. "Business Services, the Regions and Regional Policy", *Regional Studies*, 19, 4, pp.353-63.

_____, 1985b. "Services in a Postindustrial Economy", *Environment and Planning A*, 17, pp.1155-67.

_____, 1988. *Services and Uneven Development*. New York: Oxford University Press.

Marshall, J.N. and J. Bachtler, 1987. "Services and Regional Policy", *Regional Studies*, 21, 5, pp.471-75.

Marshall, J.N., P. Damesick and P. Wood, 1985. "Understanding the Location and Role of Producer Services", paper presented at the annual meeting of the Regional Science Association, Manchester, September.

Massey, D., 1984. *Spatial Divisions of Labour*. London: Macmillan.

McRae, J.J., 1985. "Can Growth in the Service Sector Rescue Western Canada?", *Canadian Public Policy*, Supplement, II, pp.351-53.

McRae, J.J. and M. Desbois, 1988. *Traded and Non-traded Services: Theory, Measurement and Policy*. Halifax: The Institute for Research on Public Policy.

_____, 1987. "The Service Sector in Vancouver: Profile, Problems and Potential." Discussion Paper, Victoria, B.C.: Institute for Research on Public Policy

Melvin, J.R., 1987. "The Role of Services in a Small Regional Economy." Discussion Paper. Victoria, B.C.: Institute for Research on Public Policy.

Melvin, J.R., 1989. *Trade in Services: A Theoretical Analysis*. Halifax: Institute for Research on Public Policy.

Moss, M.L., 1987. "Telecommunications, World Cities, and Urban Policy", *Urban Studies*, 24, pp.534-46.

Moss, M.L. and A. Dunau, 1986. *The Location of Back Offices: Emerging Trends and Development Patterns.* New York: Real Estate Institute, New York University.

Nelson, K., 1986. "Labour Demand, Labour Supply and the Suburbanization of Low-Wage Office Work", in A. Scott and M. Storper (eds.), *Production, Work, and Territory.* Boston: Allen and Unwin.

Netherlands Economic Institute, 1986. *Telecommunications and the Location of Producer Services in the Netherlands.* Brussels: Commission of the European Communities, FAST Occasional Paper 98.

Netzer, D., 1977. "The Economic Future of Cities: Winners and Losers", *New York Affairs*, 4, 4, pp.81-93.

Norrie, K. and M. Percy, 1988. "Services and Regional Economic Performance: An Exploratory Analysis". Discussion Paper. Victoria, B.C.: Institute for Research on Public Policy.

North, D.C., 1955. "Locational Theory and Regional Economic Growth". *Journal of Political Economy*, 63, pp.243-58.

_____, 1956. "A Reply". *Journal of Political Economy*, 64, pp.165-68.

Northern Region Strategy Team, 1977. *Strategic Plan for the Northern Region, Volume 2: Economic Development Policy.* London: HMSO.

Noyelle, T.J. and T.M. Stanback, 1984. *The Economic Transformation of American Cities.* Totawa, NJ: Rowman & Allanheld.

Ontario, 1986. *Ontario Study of the Service Sector.* Toronto: Ministry of Treasury and Economics, Government of Ontario.

Picot, W.G., 1986. *Canada's Industries: Growth in Jobs over Three Decades.* Ottawa: Minister of Supply and Services.

Philippe, J., 1984. "Les services aux entreprises et la politique de développement régional", paper presented at the annual meeting of l'Association de science régionale de langue française, Lugano, Switzerland, August.

Philippe, J. and M.C. Monnoyer, 1985. "L'interaction entre les prestations de service et le développement régional". Centre d'économie régionale, Aix-en-Provence.

Polèse, M., 1981. "Interregional Service Flows: Economic Integration and Regional Policy: Some Considerations Based on Canadian Survey Data", *Revue d'economie régionale et urbaine*, 4, pp.51-73.

Polèse, M. and J. Léger, 1982. *Montréal, centre de services aux enterprises et métropole québécoise*. Montréal: École des Hautes Commerciales de Montréal, centre d'études en administration internationale.

Porat, M., 1977. *The Information Economy: Definition and Measurement*. Washington, D.C.: U.S. Department of Commerce, Office of Telecommunications Special Publication 77-12(1).

Pye, R., 1979. "Office Location: The Role of Communications and Technology". In P.W. Daniels (ed.), *Spatial Patterns of Office Growth and Location*. Chichester: Wiley & Sons, pp.239-76.

Richardson, P.R., 1987. "Exporting Natural Resource Expertise From Canada". Unpublished manuscript presented to the Third Banff Conference on Natural Resources Law, Banff, Alberta.

Reifler, R.F., 1976. "Implications of Service Industry Growth for Regional Development Strategies", *Annals of Regional Science*, 10, pp.88-104.

Ryan, C., 1987. "Trade in the Presence of Endogenous Intermediation in an Asymmetric World". Discussion Paper. Victoria, B.C.: Institute for Research on Public Policy.

Scott, A.J., 1988. *New Industrial Spaces*. London: Pion.

Shelp, R.K., 1981. *Beyond Industrialization: An Ascendance of Global Service Economy*. New York: Praeger.

Smith, A., 1925. *An Inquiry into the Nature and Causes of the Wealth of Nations*. London: Methuen.

Stanback, T.M., P.J. Bearse, T.J. Noyelle and R.A. Karasek, 1981. *Services: The New Economy*. Totawa, NJ: Rowman & Allanheld.

Statistics Canada, *Service Industries in the Business Sector*, Volume 1 of Statistics Canada Documentation of Services.

_____, 1988. *Quarterly Estimates of the Canadian Balance of International Payments*. Catalogue No. 67-001.

Statistics Canada, 1986. *Canada's International Trade in Services*. Catalogue No. 67-510.

Stigler, G., 1956. *Trends in Employment in the Service Industries*. Princeton, N.J.: Princeton University Press.

Swan, N.M., 1985. "The Service Sector: Engine of Growth?", *Canadian Public Policy*, Supplement, II, pp.344-50.

Tornqvist, G., 1970. *Contact Systems and Regional Development.* Lund: Lund Studies in Geography (B), no. 35, University of Lund.

Tiebout, C.M., 1962. *The Community Economic Base Study. New York: Committee on Economic Development.*

Tschettler, J., 1987. "Producer Services Industries: Why Are They Growing So Rapidly?" *Monthly Labor Review*, Dec. pp.31-40.

Van Haselen, H., W. Molle and R. De Wit, 1985. "Technological Change and Service Employment in the Regions of Europe: The Case of Banking and Insurance", paper presented at the conference on Technological Change and Employment, Zandvoort, Netherlands, March.

Verreault, R. and M. Polèse, 1989. *L'exportation de services par les firmes canadiennes de génie-conseil : évolution récente et avantages concurrentiels.* Halifax: Institute for Research on Public Policy.

Walker, R.A., 1985. "Is There A Service Economy? The Changing Capitalist Division of Labour", *Science and Society*, 49, pp.42-83.

Wallis, J. and D. North, 1986. *Measuring the Transaction Sector in the American Economy 1870–1970.* Unpublished manuscript.

Webber, M.M., 1973. "Urbanization and Communications", in G. Gerbner, L.P. Gross and W.H. Melody (eds.), *Communications Technology and Social Policy.* New York: John Wiley & Sons.

Wheeler, J.O., 1988. "The Corporate Role of Large Metropolitan Areas in the United States", *Growth and Change*, 19, 2, pp.75-86.

Appendix A

Composition of Synthetic Regions

Region Type 1: 300,000 +

Region	Province
Quebec	Quebec
Montreal	Quebec
Ottawa-Hull	Ontario
Toronto	Ontario
Hamilton	Ontario
St. Catharines-Niagara	Ontario
Winnipeg	Manitoba
Calgary	Alberta
Edmonton	Alberta
Vancouver	British Columbia

10 units

Region Type 2: 100,000 - 300,000

Region	Province
St. John's	Newfoundland
Halifax	Nova Scotia
Saint John	New Brunswick
Chicoutimi-Jonquiere	Quebec
Sherbrooke	Quebec
Trois-Rivières	Quebec
Kingston	Ontario
Oshawa	Ontario
Kitchener	Ontario
London	Ontario
Windsor	Ontario
Sudbury	Ontario
Thunder Bay	Ontario
Regina	Saskatchewan
Saskatoon	Saskatchewan
Victoria	British Columbia

16 units

Region Type 3: 50,001 - 100,000 central

Region	Province
Fredericton	New Brunswick
Shawinigan	Quebec
Drummondville	Quebec
Saint-Jean-sur-Richelieu	Quebec
Cornwall	Quebec
Peterborough	Ontario
Brantford	Ontario
Guelph	Ontario
Sarnia	Ontario
Barrie	Ontario
Nanaimo	British Columbia

11 units

Region Type 4: 50,001 - 100,000 peripheral

Region	Province
Sydney	Nova Scotia
Moncton	New Brunswick
North Bay	Ontario
Sault Ste. Marie	Ontario
Kelowna	British Columbia
Kamloops	British Columbia
Prince George	British Columbia
Lethbridge	Alberta

8 units

Region Type 5: 25,001 - 50,000 central

Region	Province
Truro	Nova Scotia
Thetford Mines	Quebec
Victoriaville	Quebec
Granby	Quebec
Saint-Hyacinthe	Quebec
Sorel	Quebec
Joliette	Quebec
Salaberry-de-Valleyfield	Quebec
Saint-Jerome	Quebec
Brockville	Ontario
Belleville	Ontario
Trenton	Ontario
Stratford	Ontario
Chatham	Ontario
Orillia	Ontario
Moose Jaw	Saskatchewan
Chilliwack	British Columbia
Newcastle	Ontario
Alma	Quebec

19 units

Region Type 6: 25,001 - 50,000 peripheral

Region	Province
Corner Brook	Newfoundland
Charlottetown	Prince Edward Island
New Glasgow	Nova Scotia
Sydney Mines	Nova Scotia
Rimouski	Quebec
Baie-Comeau	Quebec
Sept-Iles	Quebec
Rouyn	Quebec
Owen Sound	Ontario
Midland	Ontario
Prince Albert	Saskatchewan
Medicine Hat	Alberta
Vernon	British Columbia
Port Alberni	British Columbia
Courtenay	British Columbia
Terrace	British Columbia
Red Deer	Alberta
Timmins	Ontario
Brandon	Manitoba
Fort McMurray	Alberta

20 units

Region Type 7: 10,001 - 25,000 central

Region	Province
Carbonear	Newfoundland
Kentville	Nova Scotia
Oromocto	New Brunswick
Dolbeau	Quebec
Saint-Georges	Quebec
Magog	Quebec
Asbestos	Quebec
Lachute	Quebec
Hawkesbury	Ontario
Smiths Falls	Ontario
Cobourg	Ontario
Lindsay	Ontario
Fergus	Ontario
Leamington	Ontario
Portage la Prairie	Manitoba

Montmagny	Quebec
Cowansville	Quebec

17 units

Region Type 8: 10,001 - 25,000 peripheral

Region	Province
Chibougamau	Quebec
Labrador City	Newfoundland
Bathurst	New Brunswick
Campbellton	New Brunswick
Edmundston	New Brunswick
Rivière-du-Loup	Quebec
La Tuque	Quebec
Val-d'Or	Quebec
Pembroke	Ontario
Petawawa	Ontario
Haileybury	Ontario
Kenora	Ontario
Thompson	Manitoba
Swift Current	Saskatchewan
North Battleford	Saskatchewan
Trail	British Columbia
Powell River	British Columbia
Prince Rupert	British Columbia
Matane	Quebec

19 units

Region Type 9: < 10,000 central

Region	Province
Division 1	Newfoundland
Colchester County	Nova Scotia
Halifax County	Nova Scotia
Hants County	Nova Scotia
Kings County	Nova Scotia
Lunenburg County	Nova Scotia
Albert County	New Brunswick
Charlotte County	New Brunswick

Kings County	New Brunswick
Queens County	New Brunswick
Saint-John County	New Brunswick
Sunbury County	New Brunswick
York County	New Brunswick
Argenteuil	Quebec
Athabaska	Quebec
Bagot	Quebec
Beauce	Quebec
Beauharnois	Quebec
Bellechasse	Quebec
Berthier	Quebec
Brome	Quebec
Champlain	Quebec
Charlevoix-est	Quebec
Charlevoix-ouest	Quebec
Chateauguay	Quebec
Deux-Montagnes	Quebec
Dorchester	Quebec
Drummond	Quebec
Frontenac	Quebec
Gatineau	Quebec
Huntingdon	Quebec
Iberville	Quebec
Joliette	Quebec
Labelle	Quebec
Lac-Saint-Jean-est	Quebec
Laprairie	Quebec
L'assomption	Quebec
Levis	Quebec
Lotbiniere	Quebec
Maskinonge	Quebec
Megantic	Quebec
Missisquoi	Quebec
Montcalm	Quebec
Montmagny	Quebec
Montmorency No. 1	Quebec
Montmorency No. 2	Quebec
Napierville	Quebec
Nicolet	Quebec
Portneuf	Quebec
Richelieu	Quebec
Richmond	Quebec
Rouville	Quebec
Saint-Hyacinthe	Quebec
Saint-Jean	Quebec
Saint-Maurice	Quebec

	Shefford	Quebec
	Sherbrooke	Quebec
	Soulanges	Quebec
	Stanstead	Quebec
	Terrebonne	Quebec
	Vaudreuil	Quebec
	Vercheres	Quebec
	Wolfe	Quebec
	Yamaska	Quebec
	Brant County	Ontario
	Dufferin County	Ontario
	Dundas County	Ontario
†	Durham Regional Municipality	Ontario
	Elgin County	Ontario
	Essex County	Ontario
	Frontenac County	Ontario
	Glengarry County	Ontario
	Grenville County	Ontario
	Grey County	Ontario
†	Haldimand-Norfolk Regional	Ontario
	Hastings County	Ontario
	Huron County	Ontario
	Kent County	Ontario
	Lambton County	Ontario
	Lanark County	Ontario
	Leeds County	Ontario
	Lennox and Addington County	Ontario
†	Manitoulin District	Ontario
	Middlesex County	Ontario
†	Niagara Regional Municipality	Ontario
	Northumberland County	Ontario
	Oxford County	Ontario
†	Peel Regional Municipality	Ontario
	Peterborough County	Ontario
	Prescott County	Ontario
	Prince Edward County	Ontario
	Russell County	Ontario
	Simcoe County	Ontario
	Stormont County	Ontario
†	Sudbury District	Ontario
†	Sudbury Regional Municipality	Ontario
†	Thunder Bay District	Ontario
	Victoria County	Ontario
†	Waterloo Regional Municipality	Ontario
	Wellington County	Ontario
†	York Regional Municipality	Ontario
	Division 1	Manitoba

Division 2	Manitoba
Division 3	Manitoba
Division 9	Manitoba
Division 10	Manitoba
Division 12	Manitoba
Division 13	Manitoba
Division 14	Manitoba
Division 2	Saskatchewan
Division 6	Saskatchewan
Division 11	Saskatchewan
Division 12	Saskatchewan
Division 15	Saskatchewan
Division 5	Alberta
Division 6	Alberta
Division 9	Alberta
Division 11	Alberta
Division 13	Alberta
Capital Regional District	British Columbia
Central Fraser Valley	British Columbia
Cowichan Valley Regional	British Columbia
Dewdney-Alouette Regional	British Columbia
Fraser-Cheam Regional	British Columbia
Nanaimo Okanagan Regional	British Columbia
Sunshine Coast Regional	British Columbia

127 units

Region Type 10: < 10,000 peripheral*

Region	Province
† Grand Falls	Newfoundland
† Summerside	Prince Edward Island
† Flin Flon	Manitoba
Division 2	Newfoundland
Division 3	Newfoundland
Division 4	Newfoundland
Division 5	Newfoundland
Division 6	Newfoundland
Division 7	Newfoundland
Division 8	Newfoundland
Division 9	Newfoundland
Division 10	Newfoundland
Kings County	Prince Edward Island
Prince County	Prince Edward Island

Queens County	Prince Edward Island
Annapolis County	Nova Scotia
Antigonish County	Nova Scotia
Cape Breton County	Nova Scotia
Cumberland County	Nova Scotia
Digby County	Nova Scotia
Guysborough County	Nova Scotia
Inverness County	Nova Scotia
Pictou County	Nova Scotia
Queens County	Nova Scotia
Richmond County	Nova Scotia
Shelburne County	Nova Scotia
Victoria County	Nova Scotia
Yarmouth County	Nova Scotia
Carleton County	New Brunswick
Gloucester County	New Brunswick
Kent County	New Brunswick
Madawaska County	New Brunswick
Northumberland County	New Brunswick
Restigouche County	New Brunswick
Victoria County	New Brunswick
Westmorland County	New Brunswick
Abitibi	Quebec
Bonaventure	Quebec
Chicoutimi	Quebec
Gaspé-est	Quebec
Gaspé-ouest	Quebec
Iles-de-la-madeleine	Quebec
Kamouraska	Quebec
Lac-Saint-Jean-ouest	Quebec
L'Islet	Quebec
Matane	Quebec
Matapedia	Quebec
Papineau	Quebec
Pontiac	Quebec
Rimouski	Quebec
Rivière-du-Loup	Quebec
Saguenay	Quebec
Temiscamingue	Quebec
Temiscouata	Quebec
Territoire-du-nouveau-Quebec	Quebec
† Algoma District	Ontario
Bruce County	Ontario
† Cochrane District	Ontario
Haliburton County	Ontario
Kenora County	Ontario
† Muskoka District Municipality	Ontario

†	Nipissing District	Ontario
	Parry Sound County	Ontario
†	Rainy River District	Ontario
	Renfrew County	Ontario
	Timiskaming County	Ontario
	Division 4	Manitoba
	Division 5	Manitoba
	Division 6	Manitoba
	Division 7	Manitoba
	Division 8	Manitoba
	Division 15	Manitoba
	Division 16	Manitoba
	Division 17	Manitoba
	Division 18	Manitoba
	Division 19	Manitoba
	Division 20	Manitoba
	Division 21	Manitoba
	Division 22	Manitoba
	Division 23	Manitoba
	Division 1	Saskatchewan
	Division 3	Saskatchewan
	Division 4	Saskatchewan
	Division 5	Saskatchewan
	Division 7	Saskatchewan
	Division 8	Saskatchewan
	Division 9	Saskatchewan
	Division 10	Saskatchewan
	Division 13	Saskatchewan
	Division 14	Saskatchewan
	Division 16	Saskatchewan
	Division 17	Saskatchewan
	Division 18	Saskatchewan
	Division 1	Alberta
	Division 2	Alberta
	Division 3	Alberta
	Division 4	Alberta
	Division 7	Alberta
	Division 8	Alberta
	Division 10	Alberta
	Division 12	Alberta
	Division 14	Alberta
	Division 15	Alberta
	Bulkey-Nechako Regional District	British Columbia
	Cariboo Regional District	British Columbia
	Central Coast Regional District	British Columbia
	Central Kootenay Regional	British Columbia
	Central Okanagan Regional	British Columbia

Columbia-Shuswap Regional	British Columbia
Comox-Strathcona Regional	British Columbia
East Kootenay Regional	British Columbia
Fraser-Fort George Regional	British Columbia
Kitimat-Stikine Regional	British Columbia
Kootenay Boundary Regional	British Columbia
Mount Waddington Regional	British Columbia
North Okanagan Regional	British Columbia
Okanagan-Similkameen Regional	British Columbia
Peace River-Liard Regional	British Columbia
Skeena-Queen Charlotte	British Columbia
Squamish-Lillooet Regional	British Columbia
Stikine Region	British Columbia
Thompson-Nicola Regional	British Columbia
Yukon	Yukon
Baffin Regional	Northwest Territories
Central Arctic Region	Northwest Territories
Forth Smith Region	Northwest Territories
Inuvik Region	Northwest Territories
Keewatin Region	Northwest Territories

127 units

* Note: In the case of region types 9 and 10, unless marked with a †
symbol, the spatial units represent census divisions. In
certain instances, these units actually represent the residual resulting from the subtraction of all of the municipal
units listed in region types 1 - 8 from the census division.
In region type 9, for example, "Halifax County" represents
the rural portion of the Halifax County census division,
resulting from the subtraction of the Halifax C.M.A. from
the census division. All data were compiled using special
runs of the 1971 and 1981 censuses, adjusted so as to
control for boundary changes between the two census
years.

Appendix B

Details on Non Respondents and Sample Selection Information

Table B.1 shows the gross[1] response rate for the mail-out and interview questionnaires where establishments are disaggregated by three types of organizational status. The classification of establishments by organizational status for the mail and interview questionnaires is based on information contained on the raw data tape while the classification for completed questionnaires and accepted interviews is taken directly from data reported by the establishment. For both data collection instruments, three establishments did not report their organization status. Measured as a percentage of total contacts, the interview questionnaire was more productive than the mail-out version for all organizational structures. Branch offices had the worst response rate for the mail-out questionnaire, but the best one for the interview version.

---

1. Establishments who could not reasonably be expected to respond because they are not service producers, or because the address obtained from the original data base was incorrect have been netted out of the analysis.

Table B.1
Response Rates for the Interview and
Questionnaire Samples by Organization Status

Status	Mail Questionnaire			Interview Questionnaire		
	Sent	Completed	%	Requested	Accepted	%
Branch Office	901	84	9.3	92	47	51.1
Head Office	327	42	12.8	165	50	30.3
Locally Owned	1,635	201	12.3	171	68	39.8
Missing Information	--	3	--	--	3	--
TOTAL	2,863	330	11.5	428	168	39.3

Table B.2 displays the gross response rates for the two samples when the data are disaggregated by the number of employees. Since employment data are taken from the raw data tape for the two populations, but from the actual questionnaire for the samples, there again may be some bias contained in the individual percentage response rates. For example, an extreme situation occurs for firms between 101/250 and 251/500 employees. None were included in the population targeted to receive the mail questionnaire, but six returned questionnaires reporting employment figures within these ranges. Obviously, the raw data base had classified these establishments in some other (perhaps out-of-date) employment category. The most important observation contained in these data is that small establishments, i.e., those with 1 - 5 employees, have very high relative response rates in comparison to the larger firms.

Finally, Table B.3 shows the gross response rates by service sector. For the mail-out questionnaire, the business services group produced the best gross response rate, while transportation/communications generated the best response to the request for a personal interview. The relatively poor response rate for the services incidental and construction sectors to both types of data collection techniques is worth further investigation.

It is also important to assess the quality of the data gathered, specifically to see how closely the population of establishments generated by the two data collection instruments profiled the universe of Vancouver-based service establishments. Recall that the population was created by randomly selecting from the universe of establishments:

Table B.2
Response Rates for the Interview and
Questionnaire Samples by Number of Employees

Status	Mail Questionnaire			Interview Questionnaire		
	Sent	Completed	%	Requested	Accepted	%
1 - 5	356	62	17.4	43	28	65.1
6 - 10	773	77	10.0	88	23	26.1
11 - 25	1,093	101	9.2	94	37	39.4
26 - 50	436	59	13.5	36	24	66.7
51 - 100	201	23	11.4	17	10	58.8
101 - 250	0	5*	--	97	32	33.0
251 - 500	0	1*	--	33	6	18.2
500 and up	4	2	50	20	7	35.0
Missing Information	--	2		--	1	
Total	2,863	330	11.5	428	168	39.3

* Due to re-classification of establishments from the original data base.

- 1 in 20 establishments with 1 to 5 employees, a 5 percent rule;
- 1 in 2 establishments with 6 to 10 employees, a 50 percent rule;
- all establishments with 11 or more employees

This selection process had three major consequences on the distribution of the population in comparison to the universe.[2] As can be seen from Table B.4, the population contains a lower percentage of small establishments; a lower percentage of establishments in the services incidental and business services categories and a lower percentage of locally owned establishments. The universe of service establishments is characterized by a large percentage of locally owned

2. Information on the number of employees, organizational status and SIC code for the samples produced by the mail and interview questionnaires are taken directly from the survey instruments. Thus, differences in the distribution of establishments between the sample and the universe may, in part, be caused by inaccuracies in the original data base, or simply changes which have taken place in the establishment's organization structure or number of employees.

small establishments. Therefore, by selecting small establishments on a random 5 percent or 50 percent rule, we are forced to accept the fact that entries in these two categories will be underrepresented in the population.

Table B.3
Response Rates for the Interview and
Questionnaire Samples by Sector

	Mail Questionnaire			Interview Questionnaire		
Status	Sent	Completed	Percent	Requested	Accepted	Percent
Services Incidental	122	8	6.6	20	5	25.0
Construction	82	5	6.1	16	4	25.0
Transportation/ Communications	616	60	9.7	92	54	58.7
FIRE	672	83	12.4	66	25	37.9
Business Services	1371	174	12.7	234	80	34.2
Total	2863	330	11.5	428	168	39.3

Table B.4 also profiles the sample produced by means of the mail-out and interview questionnaire techniques. The sample generated by the interview technique is overrepresentative of the large establishments, and underrepresents the very small ones (1-5 employees). This follows naturally from the fact that large establishments are easier to contact, and are less likely to have gone out of business or moved. The interviews also produced a sample which overrepresents establishments in the transportation and communications sector, and is slightly underrepresentative of FIRE establishments. Finally, with respect to ownership status of the establishment, the sample and universe data are not strictly comparable, because the interview questionnaire used a six category system, while the information contained on the raw data tape uses only three. However, it appears that the interview sample underrepresents the category locally-owned, and overrepresents the head office and affiliated categories. The reason for the underrepresentation of locally-owned establishments is that they are also small, and hence, subject to the random sampling

Table B.4
Profile of Sample Establishments Generated by the Mail-Out and Interview Techniques

	Distribution of Universe (%)	Distribution of Population (%)	Distribution of Mail Questionnaire Sample (%)	Distribution of Interview Questionnaire Sample (%)
	(N = 11,822)	(N = 3,333)	(n = 330)	(n = 168)
Service Sector				
Services Incidental	7.1	4.4	2.4	3.0
Construction	2.4	3.0	1.5	2.4
Transp. & Comm.	15.1	21.5	18.2	32.1
FIRE	20.0	22.4	25.2	14.9
Business Services	55.3	48.8	52.7	47.6
No. of Employees				
1-5	68.4	12.1	18.8	16.6
6-10	14.2	26.1	23.3	13.7
11-25	10.2	36.0	30.6	22.0
26-50	3.9	13.8	17.3	14.3
51-100	1.9	6.6	7.0	6.0
101-250	1.0	3.4	1.5	19.0
251-500	0.3	1.1	0.3	3.6
500 and Up+	0.2	0.8	0.6	4.2
Missing Information			0.6	0.6
Organizational Structure				
Locally owned	73.6	55.1	52.4	34.5
Locally owned (linked)			8.8	6.0
HQ Cdn.	8.0	15.0	11.8	28.0
HQ Foreign			0.6	1.8
Affiliated Cdn.	18.4	29.9	22.1	19.6
Affiliated Foreign			3.3	8.3
Missing Information			0.9	1.8

Locally owned	=	Locally-owned establishment, with no affiliates or branches.
Locally owned (linked)	=	Locally-owned establishment, but linked to a larger organization or network (partnership, franchise, etc.)
HQ Cdn	=	head office with branches or affiliates of a Canadian controlled establishment or organization
HQ Foreign	=	Canadian head office of a foreign controlled establishment or organization
Affiliated Cdn	=	affiliated establishment of a Canadian controlled establishment or organization
Affiliated Foreign	=	affiliated establishment, branch or subsidiary of a foreign controlled establishment or organization

rules. Head offices are overrepresented because many are also in the transportation and communication sector, and this is an over-represented sector in the analysis.

For the sample generated by the mail-out questionnaire, the same bias against small establishments, and in favour of large ones, exists for the same reasons as discussed for the interview. The profile of establishments when sorted by SIC code and organizational status is, however, closer to the universe for the mail-out sample.

Despite our attempts to produce statistically robust estimates of service sector activity in the Vancouver region, the poor response rate to the mail-out questionnaire was a frustrating development. The low number of completed questionnaires made it difficult to investigate issues requiring detailed disaggregation of the data set because the resulting number of observations was often too small to produce generalizable results. As a consequence, it must be concluded that many of the observations made in the next section cannot be assigned levels of statistical confidence. However, the fact that the interview results, in most cases, confirmed the point made by the mail-out questionnaire data gives us subjective confidence that the conclusions being drawn are robust.

Finally, it is readily apparent for both data collection instruments, that the services incidental to the primary sector and construction categories produced such a small number of observations that further analysis could not possibly produce meaningful results. As a consequence, both categories were dropped from the analysis.

Related Publications

Order Address

The Institute for Research on Public Policy
P.O. Box 3670 South
Halifax, Nova Scotia
B3J 3K6

1-800-565-0659 (toll free)

James J. McRae and
Martine M. Desbois, eds.

*Traded and Non-traded Services: Theory,
Measurement and Policy.* 1988 $22.00
ISBN 0-88645-066-7

Roger Verreault et
Mario Polèse

*L'exportation de services par les firmes
canadiennes de génie-conseil : évolution
récente et avantages concurrentiels.* 1989
19,95 $
ISBN 0-88645-078-0

Mario Polèse,
Julie Archambault,
Marcel Gaudreau et
Roger Verreault

*Les exportations de services de gestion et de
promotion immobilières : sur quoi repose
l'avantage concurrentiel des firmes
canadiennes?* 1989 19,95 $
ISBN 0-88645-093-4

James Melvin

Trade in Services: A Theoretical Analysis.
1989 $24.95
ISBN 0-88645-090-X

PLUS: Some 40 overview and discussion papers are also available. Discussion papers cost $7.50 each, or $200.00 for the set. Overviews cost $15.00 each. A complete set of papers and overviews is available for $250.00. For the complete list, please write to the address shown above.

The Institute for Research on Public Policy
L'Institut de recherches politiques

A national, independent, research organization
Un organisme de recherche national et indépendant

Créé en 1972, l'Institut de recherches politiques est un organisme national dont l'indépendance et l'autonomie sont assurées grâce aux revenus provenant d'un fonds de dotation auquel souscrivent les gouvernements fédéral et provinciaux ainsi que le secteur privé. L'Institut obtient en outre des subventions et des contrats des gouvernements, des compagnies et des fondations afin de réaliser certains projets de recherche.

La raison d'être de l'Institut est triple :

- Servir de catalyseur au sein de la collectivité nationale en favorisant un débat public éclairé sur les principales questions d'intérêt général.

- Stimuler la participation de tous les éléments de la collectivité nationale à l'élaboration de la politique d'État.

- Trouver des solutions réalisables aux importants problèmes d'ordre politique afin de contribuer à l'élaboration d'une saine politique d'État.

L'Institut fonctionne de manière décentralisée et retient les services de chercheurs en divers points du Canada, s'assurant ainsi que toutes les régions contribuent aux recherches.

L'Institut cherche à favoriser, dans la mesure du possible, la compréhension et la discussion publiques des questions d'envergure nationale, controversées ou non. Il publie les conclusions de ses recherches avec clarté et impartialité. Les recommandations ou les conclusions énoncées dans les publications de l'Institut sont strictement celles de l'auteur et n'engagent aucunement le Conseil d'administration ou les bailleurs de fonds.

Le président assume la responsabilité ultime de publier un manuscrit au nom de l'Institut. Il jouit à cette fin des conseils du personnel de l'Institut et de critiques de l'extérieur quant à l'exactitude et à l'objectivité du texte. Ne sont publiés que les textes qui traitent de façon compétente d'un sujet digne de la réflexion du public.

Service Industries in Regional Development

by
William J. Coffey and James J. McRae

This study contains three distinct elements. First, a conceptual analysis of the locational characteristics of service industries is set out. Second, a detailed empirical analysis of the service sector in Canada using employment and occupational data from the 1971 and 1981 censuses, and questionnaire results obtained from service producing establishments, is summarized. Finally, an analysis of the policy issues relevant to service industries in regional development, especially the limited role of policy variables in decentralizing the so-called "propulsive" service industries away from the large urban centres or their immediate suburbs, is developed.

ISBN 0-88645-103-5

The Institute for Research on Public Policy
L'Institut de recherches politiques
A national, independent, research organization
Un organisme de recherche national et indépendant